Nicolas Appert

A Biography of

Nicolas Appert

1749 – 1841

by
Malcolm Summers

About the author:

Malcolm Summers graduated from London University with a degree in mathematics and has taught in secondary schools for over 30 years. Originally from Birmingham, he lives in Reading with three descendants of Nicolas Appert. In 2013 he completed and published "History of Greyfriars Church, Reading."

Published by Downs Way Publishing
1 Downs Way, Tilehurst, Reading RG31 6SL

ISBN 978-0-9927515-2-4

Photographs are by the author unless otherwise acknowledged.

Front cover:
From a drawing by Henry Cheffer (1955) – see p167

Dedication:

To three direct descendants
of Nicolas Appert

My wife and children:
Cathy, Eddie and Ellie

And in memory of Nicolas Appert's
great–great–great granddaughter

my mother-in-law
Gilberte Andrews
(née Chaudoye)

Chapter	Page

Nicolas Appert

From "*Les Artisans Illustres*"
By Édouard Foucaud[1]

A Poor Man's Burial

The last days of May 1841 were difficult. Unbearable heat was followed by violent thunderstorms. It was hard enough for those who were active and healthy; it must have been torment for the dying old man at *N° 99 Grande Rue* in Massy, south of Paris.

Nicolas Appert lingered on until the Tuesday evening, 1 June. The local priest was with him when he died, giving comfort in place of the family that were not able to be there. Everyone agreed that at least the man had lived to a good age – 91 years old! Two neighbours reported the death the next morning to the authorities at Massy Town Hall. On the Thursday, M. Appert was buried in an unmarked grave – a poor man's burial.

Two weeks later at the meeting of *La Société d'Encouragement pour l'Industrie Nationale*, Louis Jacques Thénard – a famous chemist, co-discoverer of the element boron, and later one of the 72 French scientists whose names were inscribed on the Eiffel Tower – gave a special presentation of Appert's work, calling him an "industrialist who has given birth to several developments of great value to the domestic economy and to voyages of long duration."[2]

Nicolas Appert was a man who had changed the world, not by feat of arms or by political means, but through empirical science. World famous scientists honoured his memory yet he died without the financial means to lift him above the level of sharing the common grave in Massy. How to reconcile his fame and his poverty? Nicolas Appert did not leave a Last Will and Testament, but he did leave behind a legacy in which the world has shared every day since.

Nicolas Appert's birthplace

The site of *Le Cheval Blanc*,
(The White Horse Inn)

16/18 St. John's Square,
Châlons-en-Champagne

Chapter 1

Chaalons en Champaigne: 1749 – 1772

The White Horse Inn was a large building, with total floor space greater than 1,000m[2]. It was built in an L-shape, having a ten metre frontage on St. John's Square with a gateway for coaches and a large inner courtyard. Its land extended behind the inn as far as the old town walls. There was a small 16th or 17th century house as part of the inn complex, made of wooden panelled sections. This small house, pictured opposite, is all that remains of the original inn buildings. Currently known as *N⁰ 18 place St. Jean*, this house was where the Appert family lived.

St. John's Square was a good situation for an inn. It was just off the main Paris – Metz road, near St. John's Gate in the town walls on the eastern edge of the town. *Le Cheval Blanc* would be one of the first *auberges* that the traffic from Metz, heading for the capital, came to upon arrival at Chaalons en Champaigne (now Châlons–en–Champagne).

It was here in this bustling inn that, on Monday 17 November 1749, Nicolas Appert was born.[3] He was Claude and Marie-Nicolle Appert's ninth child.

The inn had probably been in Nicolas's mother's family for over fifty years.[4] Marie-Nicolle Huet had been born at the inn in 1714[5] and no doubt she joined her parents in their work as soon as she was old enough. Both of her parents had died by the time Marie-Nicolle was in her early twenties, leaving her to continue the work of innkeeper alone.[6]

A few years later, ownership of the business passed to Claude Appert as the dowry in Claude and Marie-Nicolle's marriage contract, drawn up on 24 October 1739[7] before their marriage in nearby St. John's Church on Monday 9 November that year.[8]

Claude had been born about 1711[9] in Saint-Remy-sur-Bussy, a small village about 15 miles north-east of Châlons, to a family of farmers and ploughmen.[10] Claude's father, Jean, had inherited the family farm from his father. When Jean became too old to continue farming the land it passed to one of Claude's brothers. At some stage Claude left the family farm and moved to Châlons–en–Champagne.

"Here was built the White Horse Inn where,
on 17 November 1749,
Nicolas Appert was born,
the inventor of preserving food
by heat in a hermetically sealed container."

Commemorative Plaque affixed to *N° 18 place St. Jean,*
Châlons-en-Champagne, in 1986

The White Horse Inn faced St. John's Church across a narrow street, at the main road end of the square. The Church faces into the square, at the meeting of the three roads that frame the open space. There are several other houses dating from the 16th to 18th centuries in the local area.

St. John's Church is believed to be the oldest in Châlons. Its nave dates from about 1100 and the whole church has been excellently restored.[11] The transepts each have a pair of chapels, and there is a further small chapel that has been added onto the outside at the south-west corner. This addition, dating from the 16th century, was funded by a community of *arbalétriers*, or crossbowmen, and thus dedicated to Saint Sebastian. This small chapel houses the baptismal font.

Engraving of St. John's Church, Châlons, and St. John's Gate with the back of *l'auberge du Cheval Blanc* on the left

Leblanc 1792[12]

The Church of St. John the Baptist,
St. John's Square, Châlons-en-Champagne
Below : The Chapel of St. Sebastian at the south-west corner

Above: Nicolas's birthplace seen from the steps of
the Church of St. John the Baptist,
St. John's Square, Châlons-en-Champagne

The name of the town of Châlons came originally from the Celtic tribe of Gauls called the *Catalaunes* – thus the name of the town was Catalaunum to the Romans. Over the centuries the name went through variations: Châlons, Chaslons en Champaigne and Chaalons en Champaigne, this last being the name that Nicolas knew the town by when he lived there. At the Revolution, nearly twenty years after Nicolas had left the town, it was renamed again: Châlons–sur–Marne.

The town's name was changed once more to Châlons–en–Champagne in 1998 at the time it became the capital of the *Région Champagne – Ardenne*. Today, it is a city with a population of just under 50,000 inhabitants. At the time of Nicolas's birth, in the middle 18th century, it was home to about 12,000 people.[13]

The 12th and 13th centuries were the most prosperous times for the town. The basis of its economy was the production of very high quality woollen cloth. By the end of the thirteenth century the town boasted seventeen religious buildings, either built or re-built by then. This was also the time at which the town reached its maximum area, until spreading much wider in modern times. With the Hundred Years' War and the rise of Paris as the economic centre of gravity of northern France, Châlons's prosperity declined.

Many battles have taken place in this area with it being such a strategically important and much fought over region of France. In the 1851 book "Fifteen Decisive Battles of the World" two of the fifteen battles are in the Châlons area.[14] The first took place in 451 when Attila the Hun was defeated by the joint forces of the Roman General Aëtius and Visigoth King Theodoric I in the Battle of Châlons, otherwise known as the Battle of the Catalaunian Plains. The second was a battle from Nicolas's own time that we shall come to later.

After Marie-Nicolle and Claude's marriage in 1739, most

of the next 13 years saw an addition to the family. Their first eight children were Louis-Gervais,[15] Marie-Anne,[16] then twins Augustin and Margueritte,[17] followed by Marie-Margueritte,[18] Jules-Claude-Marie, [19] Louis-Etienne[20] and then Marie-Reine.[21] Sadly twins Augustin and Margueritte, and Louis-Etienne all died in infancy, and Marie-Anne died aged 7.

We therefore come to the point when their ninth child, Nicolas, was born in November 1749, joining surviving siblings Louis-Gervais, who was 9 years old, Margueritte aged 6, Jules-Claude-Marie 3 and Marie-Reine 1.

Nicolas was baptised in this font
in the Chapel of St. Sebastian,
St. John the Baptist Church,
Châlons-en-Champagne

Baby Nicolas was baptised on the day of his birth in the *Chapelle St. Sébastien* in St. John's Church. The custom of the day was that the midwife would carry the newborn from the house to the door of the church, where she would hand over the baby to the godparents, who had the privilege of declaring the name of the baby. Marie-Nicolle would have stayed at home, well cared for by servants in the inn.

The parish priest, Abbé Gellé, conducted the ceremony and completed the parish register of baptisms, marriages and funerals:

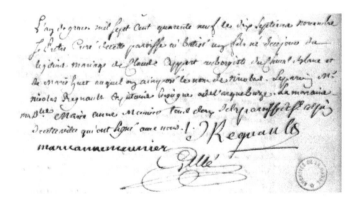

Baptism entry for Nicolas Appert[22]

The year of grace 1749, 17 November, I, priest of this parish, have baptised a boy born today of the legal marriage of Claude Appert, innkeeper of the White Horse, and of Marie Huet, to whom is given the name Nicolas. The godfather M. Nicolas Regnaud, Captain-ensign of *L'Arquebuse*, the godmother Miss Marie-Anne Meunier, both of the parish of St. Alpin in this town and who have signed with us. Gellé.

This baptismal entry was first tracked down by René Gandhilon in 1943 in the *Archives départementales de la Marne*.[23] The entry shows that Nicolas did not have any other names at his baptism – in various modern versions of his name he has gained the middle name of François. The baptism record may not be definitive, however, since, for example, Nicolas's brother Jean-Baptiste is recorded as simply Jean on his baptismal record.[24]

On 20 June 1750, when Nicolas was only seven months old, his parents bought *l'Hôtel du Palais Royal* for the sum of 7,500 *louis*. The family moved to this much larger and grander inn on 1 October 1750.[25]

The Royal Palace Hotel was less than half a mile from the White Horse Inn, on the corner of *rue Saint Jacques* and Treasurer's Street. The *rue St. Jacques* is now named *rue Léon Bourgeois*, after the late nineteenth century Prime Minister of France who became the President of the League of Nations after the First World War and winner of the Nobel Peace Prize in 1920.

The Royal Palace Hotel was near the centre of the town in a much busier commercial area than St. John's Square.

Plaque at the site of
The Royal Palace
Hotel,
rue Léon Bourgeois,
Châlons-en-
Champagne

Affixed 1999

9

Above: Detail of the plaque on p9
Showing the Royal Palace Hotel
at the end of the 19th century,
renamed *L'Hôtel De La Cloche*

Below: the same site now at 2 *rue Léon Bourgeois*

Opposite the Royal Palace Hotel was the 12th century early Gothic Collegiate Church of Notre-Dame-en-Vaux, built on an original 9th century church site. The church is now the symbol of Châlons–en–Champagne and was made a World Heritage site by UNESCO in November 2000.

Church of *Notre-Dame-en-Vaux*

Viewed from the site of the Royal Palace Hotel
Châlons-en-Champagne

The church has a notable carillon of 51 bells, installed in 1864, so replacing the bells that the Appert family would have heard. The Appert family would have regularly taken mass at Notre-Dame-en-Vaux. Their tenth child, François, was baptised there on New Year's Day 1751.[26]

The Royal Palace Hotel was already very old by 1750. From 1580 until 1720 it had been called Moulinet. This name is still commemorated by a street across from the site of the Hotel: Impasse du Moulinet. The Hotel was named the Royal Palace around 1735.[27]

Restored buildings opposite the site of
The Royal Palace Hotel, *rue Léon Bourgeois.*
The *Impasse du Moulinet* is the alleyway to the right

In 1780 an inventory of *l'Hôtel du Palais Royal* was made following Claude Appert's death.[28] This gives a good description of the hotel after thirty years' ownership by the Appert family, including an extension that was carried out in 1770.

The Hotel had twenty guest rooms. Some of the rooms were very ornately furnished with satin covered armchairs and canopies over feather beds and imposing fireplaces and chimneys. There was a large internal courtyard with a gallery leading to the rooms. The hotel boasted a very large kitchen, a dining room, a huge cellar, a stable and an attic. The rooms were named rather than numbered, with sixteen called after European cities:

Berlin	Constantinople
Copenhague	Francfort
Frascati	Londres
Madrid	Manheim
Naples	Paris
Petersbourg	Rome
Stockholm	Turin
Varsovie	Vienne

Three other rooms were named using colours: white, yellow and green. The final room was described as "the small downstairs bedroom."

In the 1780 inventory there is also a full list of the contents of the cellar, which contained 1,511 bottles of wine:

1,200	white wine
103	red wine
160	sparkling wine (probably Champagne)
15	"grey wine"
33	"the colour of oat straw"

On 16 May 1752 Jean-Baptiste, the family's eleventh and last child, was born.[29] His mother Marie-Nicolle was then approaching her 38th birthday. This new addition brought the number of surviving children to seven: five boys and two girls, with the oldest aged 11 years. Nicolas was aged 2½

with two younger brothers.

It seems that tragedy was never far from the Appert family in these years. With two daughters already dead, neither of the two remaining daughters survived into adulthood. Marie-Reine died on 22 August 1754, aged 6. At the time of her death, she was at the presbytery home of her uncle François Huet,[30] her mother's brother, who was the priest at Coolus and Compertrix. This parish was a short distance along the river Marne to the south of Châlons, and the family visited there often. Marie-Reine is buried in the parish cemetery there.[31] The remaining daughter Marie-Margueritte died aged 15 in 1760.[32]

As Nicolas grew up, he was probably of small stature, with blue eyes and light brown hair, if later descriptions are anything to go by. While he was young, his uncle François taught him and his siblings the basics of reading, writing and arithmetic at Coolus.[33] When Jules-Claude-Marie was aged 10, in 1756, he went to the Jesuit College in Châlons. The College closed in 1758, so Jules was not there long. Uncle François had studied there from 1729 to 1732, and must have been pleased to send one of his nephews to his former school.

Nothing is known of any other education Nicolas received. He may well have attended a day school around the age of 10. Not too long after, however, he would be working as an apprentice in his family's Hotel, learning the trade of being an innkeeper. Nicolas learned how to brew beer and to pickle foods. His apprenticeship also included time as wine waiter, cellarman and cook. Later, Nicolas wrote of this time of apprenticeship:

> Reared in the art of preparing and preserving by these processes, I knew alimentary products; having lived, as it were, in pantries, in breweries, in storerooms, and in the cellars of Champagne, as well as in the factories of the confectioners and

distillers, and in the store-houses of the grocers; accustomed to superintend and to conduct establishments of this kind during forty-five years, I have been able to give a faithful account of my work, aided by numerous advantages which could not be procured by the majority of those who are occupied with the art of preserving foods.[34]

Nicolas also gained experience elsewhere. He worked at *La Pomme d'Or*, the Golden Apple, possibly the best known inn in Châlons. It was at *N° 56 rue de la Marne*, just 500m away from the Royal Palace Hotel, beyond the Church of Notre-Dame-en-Vaux and on past the Town Hall square.

La Pomme d'Or was host to many a famous visitor. King Gustav III of Sweden lodged there – albeit incognito, as was often the case with travelling royalty at the time – in February 1771 on his way to Paris. A few years before that, however, an incident occurred that involved the young Nicolas, aged at most 16, with the erstwhile King of Poland, Stanisław I Leszczyński, by this time Duke of Lorraine.

In or before 1766 Stanisław was travelling through Châlons, en route to visit his daughter, Marie, wife of King Louis XV of France. In Nicolas's 1813 3rd edition of his famous book, *Le livre de tous les ménages ou l'art de conserver pendant plusieurs années toutes les substances animales et végétales* (he had a way with titles!), he wrote of the incident in some detail. This was probably his first experience of recognition for his culinary skill.

> I will tell the tale of the onion soup. Although humble, there is nothing better than this well-prepared soup.
>
> The King of Poland, Stanisław, is a case in point. On one of his trips to Lunéville at Versailles, where he went each year to visit the Queen, his daughter, he stopped at an inn in Châlons where he was served an onion soup. It was so delicate and well-prepared that he would not resume his journey without having learned for himself how to prepare a similar one. Clad

in his dressing gown, His Majesty descended to the kitchen and desired the chef to work while he watched. Neither the smoke, nor the smell of the onion, which brought forth many tears, could distract his attention. He observed everything, taking many notes. He did not climb back up to his room until he was certain that he possessed the art of creating excellent onion soup.[35]

Stanisław I
Leszczyński

(October 20, 1677 –
February 23, 1766)

Twice King of Poland
1704 – 1714,
1733 – 1736

and thereafter Duke
of Lorraine[36]

Nicolas, of course, was the chef. Nicolas named his recipe *Soupe à l'oignon à la Stanislas* in the King's honour. In his book, Nicolas went on to give the recipe that the King was so keen to discover:

Remove the top crust of a loaf, break it in pieces and heat it by a fire on both sides. When these crusts are hot, rub them with fresh butter, and heat them again until they are a little roasted;

put them on a plate while frying the onions in fresh butter; ordinarily one puts in three big onions, about 100g, diced very small; leave them on the fire until slightly tinted, stirring almost continually; next add the crusts and continue stirring until the onion browns. When it is the right colour, take from the saucepan, add boiling water, seasoning and any necessary water, then leave simmering for at least a quarter of an hour before serving.

On 29 January 1770, Claude Appert, nearing 60 years of age but still successfully building the business of the Royal Palace Hotel, bought an adjoining house and shop on the Notre Dame crossroads side of the Hotel.[37] The Royal Palace Hotel was extended into this area as a result, making it even grander than before.

The Hotel's name went through several changes at the end of the 18th century. Nicolas's youngest brother, Jean-Baptiste, eventually took over the business as we shall see later. During the difficult days of the Revolution the name Royal was definitely a liability. Jean-Baptiste changed the name to *Le Palais National*. Then as things worsened, the Palace part had to be dropped too, and the hotel became "The National House." Jean-Baptiste must have been something of a rebel, because he decided, in 1797, to reinstate the Royal Palace name, saying that business had fallen off since the name was changed. Sadly, he was forced to change it again, first back to "The National Palace" and then "The Imperial Palace." In 1803 Jean-Baptiste sold the hotel, no doubt thoroughly exasperated by having to pay for new name boards on the front of the building! The new owner was Pierre-André Angoin, who had been leasing the hotel from Jean-Baptiste for nearly three years before this. Towards the end of the 19th century the hotel was renamed yet again: first to "The Bell and Palace," and lastly to *L'Hôtel De La Cloche*, "The Bell Inn." Unfortunately, the hotel was destroyed by fire in the German invasion of

17

1940.[38]

In 1769, a few hundred metres south of the Royal Palace Hotel, a large gate was erected in the old ramparts of the town. It was named the *Porte Dauphine*, in celebration of the arrival in the following year in the town of the Archduchess of Austria, Marie Antoinette, by then already married by proxy to the Dauphin, the future King Louis XVI. The proxy marriage took place at 6pm on 19 April 1770 at the Church of the Augustinian Friars in Vienna, with the Archduke Ferdinand, Marie Antoinette's elder brother, as proxy bridegroom. The advantage of a proxy wedding was that *Madame la Dauphine* could travel into France with her new status.

Porte Sainte Croix,
formerly the *Porte Dauphine*
Châlons-en-Champagne

Entering France via Strasbourg, Châlons was on the route to Paris. The fourteen year old Dauphine entered the town through the new triumphal arch on 11 May 1770. There were theatrical entertainments staged for the Dauphine's pleasure: *Partie de chasse d'Henry IV* and *Lucile*, both performed by actors from the royal household. Then there were fireworks, followed by a huge formal dinner. Marie Antoinette then had the delight of military music being played under her window at *l'Hôtel de l'Intendance*, quite probably late into the night since local residents (the Royal Palace Hotel of course included) had to have their houses lit up all night – on pain of a fine of 20 *livres*!

The next day Marie Antoinette left to continue her journey, finally meeting Louis for the first time near Compiègne. The entertainments at Châlons had cost in excess of a staggering 16 thousand *livres*.

The town of Châlons featured again in the story of the unfortunate King Louis XVI and Marie Antoinette, in June 1791 at the time of their ill-fated "flight to Varennes."

In 1771, the year following the Dauphine's visit, Nicolas decided to try to set up a brewery with Louis-Gervais and Jules-Claude-Marie, his two older brothers. They called it the *Brasserie Royale à Chaalons* (Royal Brewery of Châlons). They applied to *L'Intendant de Champagne*, Rouillé d'Orfeuil, for the title to be granted to them to trade under that name on 17 March 1772.[39]

However, the General Inspector for the region, in his reply on 4 April, refused them the title because he did not think that the establishment was important enough to merit it. The "Royal" title would have given them tax reductions on their products, and so it would have been important for their business plan and cash flow. Despite this, Louis-Gervais and Jules-Claude-Marie decided to continue to run the brewery.

However, the setback seems to have prompted Nicolas to

seek his fortune elsewhere. He packed his bags and left Châlons–en–Champagne, never to live there again, and in 1772, aged 23, he headed east for Germany.

Commemorative street not far from the site of
The Royal Palace Hotel,
Châlons-en-Champagne

Commemorative Postcard
Dated 18 December 1999

Celebrating 250 years since Appert's birth

Design by Roland Irolla (1935 –)

(From the author's collection)

Above: Ducal Palace, Zweibrücken[40]

Below: Christian IV,
Pfalzgraf und Herzog von der Pfalz,
Zweibrücken-Birkenfeld[41]

Chapter 2

In the Rhineland: 1772 – 1784

Zweibrücken is 160 miles east of Châlons–en–Champagne, with Metz approximately at the halfway point of the journey. It was the capital of the Duchy and Palatinate of Zweibrücken-Birkenfeld, an independent state in the Holy Roman Empire in what is now Germany. The Duchy and Palatinate only existed from 1731 to 1797, emerging from the combination of two states in the time of Christian III and ending its independence by being ceded to France.

The Palatinate covered just less than 1,000 square miles, roughly the same area as modern day Luxembourg, with a population of 80,000 people. Christian III died in 1735 and the title passed to his young son, Christian IV, who was then barely 13 years old. His mother, Caroline of Nassau-Saarbrücken, was regent for the young Duke until 1740.

Zweibrücken is built in a loop formed by the river Schwarzbach, and its old castle, the Karlsberg, built in 1150, could only be reached by crossing one of the two bridges that gave the town its name both in French and in German. The Zweibrücken Palace where Christian lived and held court is today the seat of the Higher Regional Court. It is an interesting hybrid: a baroque building with Nordic influence, according to the town's literature. It was built between 1720 and 1725 by Erikson Sundahl for Gustav, the Duke of Zweibrücken who preceded Christian III, the last of the Swedish Dukes. The Palace was destroyed during an air attack in 1945, but has been rebuilt from the original plans to be an exact replacement of the original.

Christian had the marvellous title of *Pfalzgraf und Herzog von der Pfalz* (Palatinate Count and Duke). He is remembered in Zweibrücken as a good-natured Duke who encouraged much grand building, making the town a more imposing capital. He also plunged the royal family into debt both by trying, unsuccessfully, to establish a porcelain business in the town, and by spending freely on his alchemy experiments.

Christian IV was a great patron of the arts, especially of French masters. He commissioned many paintings, several of them then being exhibited at the Paris Salon. In 1755 Christian founded a stud of horses, which is still known throughout the world today. Then in 1757 he created the Royal Deux-Ponts Regiment composed of both French and German soldiers.

In 1772 Nicolas took service with Christian IV, as *élève de bouche*, or catering cadet.[42] It seems a strange career move on Nicolas's part, to go so far, to a German speaking country. What attracted him to the court of Zweibrücken-Birkenfeld? How did he get his appointment?

We do not know the answer to these questions for certain, but I think that a strong possibility lies in the person of Stanisław Leszczyński, Duke of Lorraine and twice King of Poland, who enjoyed Nicolas's onion soup so much at the *Pomme d'Or*. When Nicolas met Stanisław it was towards the end of the latter's life: he died in 1766. Prior to that, during one of the several troubled periods of Stanisław's life, he lived in Zweibrücken as an honoured guest of the then ruler of the town, the King of Sweden. Stanisław lived in Zweibrücken from 1714 until 1719, building a summer residence there. He kept close ties with the town, even when it had changed hands to Christian's father and then to Christian himself.

Christian IV had married Maria Jeanne Camasse (or sometimes Gamache) in or near 1751 when he was 29 and she was only 17. Maria had been born in Strasbourg, daughter of Jean-Baptiste Camasse, an actor, and Eléonore Roux. Maria had grown up in Mainz and become a ballerina. Due to the difference in their social status, the union of Maria and Christian IV was morganatic, meaning that Maria retained her social position as a commoner and that their children could not inherit their father's estates or position.

Christian used his connections with Stanisław to improve Maria's social status. First Christian bought the *Seigneurie Forbach* in Lorraine for her. Then Stanisław, by virtue of his position as Duke of Lorraine, elevated Maria and her descendants to Counts and Countesses of Forbach. In order to make this legal, Christian and Maria had to be married again under French law, which they duly did on Saturday 3 September 1757. Their children numbered four boys and three girls by the time Nicolas joined the Duke's service in 1772.

There is at least a possibility that, after Stanisław had copied the recipe for the onion soup, he said to the talented young chef that if he wanted to gain wider experience he could give him a letter of introduction to the Ducal Court of Christian IV.

However it came about, Nicolas was *élève de bouche de la Maison ducale de Christian IV* for three years, continuing to learn his trade as he prepared food for the noble family.

In 1773 Nicolas would have had to seek permission to travel back to Châlons to celebrate his brother's wedding. Jules-Claude-Marie married Jeanne-Catherine Lamairesse on Tuesday 7 September. The ceremony took place at Coolus, with his uncle François Huet being the officiating priest.[43] Nicolas would not have been able to see his family often during this time, and so this must have been a memorable occasion.

On Sunday 5 November 1775 Christian IV died aged 53 at *Jagdschloss*, his "hunting lodge" at Pettersheim about 20 miles north of Zweibrücken. He had had a hunting accident and did not recover. He was buried in the 15th century *Alexanderskirche* in Zweibrücken. Since Christian's children could not inherit his titles, they passed to his brother's son, Charles II.

The Duke bequeathed Maria a huge 92,000 *livres* fortune, a Parisian house, the titles Dowager Duchess of Zweibrücken and Countess of Forbach, and her favourite residence: Strahlenheim, the château at Forbach. Maria moved permanently to her home in Forbach.

Nicolas also left Zweibrücken. He stayed with the family he had served for the last three years, relocating to Strahlenheim Château, and serving Christian's widow. By this time he had been promoted to become an *officier de Bouche*, or catering officer.[44] He stayed with Maria, Countess of Forbach, for a further nine years until 1784. Nicolas was by the end of that time in his 35th year.

If Nicolas had chosen instead to stay with Christian's sons, due to their posts in the Zweibrücken army he would almost certainly have found himself in America. The Regiment fought as part of Rochambeau's expeditionary corps alongside American forces in the War of Independence. The Royal Deux-Ponts Regiment under Christian as Colonel in Chief and second-in-command William stormed and captured Yorktown, Virginia, in 1781, losing 29 men but achieving the surrender of the 8,000 British garrison. Yorktown and Zweibrücken have been "twin towns" since 1978.

Nicolas's move took him back to France. Forbach lies about midway between Zweibrücken and Metz. It is now a town of 23,000 inhabitants in the Moselle Department and Region of Lorraine.

Strahlenheim Château, Forbach[45]

Strahlenheim Château is close to the centre of Forbach, not far from the Town Hall. It was built in 1716 by Comte Henning Von Strahlenheim. Various sources say that it was bought in 1775 for Maria Camasse, but it seems more likely that it would have been part of the purchase of the *Seigneurie Forbach* in the late 1750s. 1775 was when it became Maria's as her inheritance from Christian's estate.

Strahlenheim Château later became *Le Château Barrabino*, named after a mayor of the town who bought it in the Nineteenth Century. It is now the Club Barrabino, boasting a pool and a gym, as well as conference facilities. In front of the Château, between the *rue du Château* and the main road *Avenue Saint Rémy*, is the *place Nicolas Appert*.

After three years in the bustle and busy atmosphere of Zweibrücken, Nicolas probably enjoyed the smaller household at Forbach. Perhaps he could work with a little more finesse for the table of the Countess. Maria enjoyed entertaining and being entertained by theatre groups and musicians. She held lavish balls, huge festivals and hunts in the local forests.[46] In all these events Nicolas's talents must have played a prominent part.

Maria stayed in her Parisian house for part of each year. It is likely that she would be accompanied by her household, especially her chef and kitchen staff. If so, then Nicolas would have gained his first experiences of the capital. He would also have presented meals for the highest nobility in Paris, as Maria was part of that set and was even a close friend of Marie Antoinette.

At least one set of Maria's correspondence has survived from this time. She became good friends with the new American Commissioner, an ambassadorial post otherwise known as the United States Minister for France. This was the highly popular Benjamin Franklin, who lived in Passy, a small suburb of Paris, from 1776 to 1785. From this correspondence, covering some dates in 1777 to 1779,[47] it seems that Maria tended to spend September to January in Paris, and then sometime before March return to Forbach. When she was in Paris she invited Benjamin Franklin to dine frequently, so no doubt Nicolas catered for these events.

In 1778 news reached Nicolas in Forbach that his younger brother François, a soldier in the famous Noailles Regiment, had died aged 27 at Châlons.[48] François was just a year younger than Nicolas and so they were bound to have been close when growing up.

There were now just four brothers surviving from the original eleven children. After the brewery business ended, Louis-Gervais had also left Châlons and was now living in Zutphen in the Netherlands, about 250 miles to the north east of Châlons. Jules-Claude-Marie had become a grocer with a shop on *rue Saint Jacques*, a short distance from *L'Hôtel du Palais Royal*. The youngest, Jean-Baptiste, was taking care of the hotel.[49]

On 27 July 1780, during the time that Nicolas was working for the Countess of Forbach, his father, Claude, died aged 69.[50] Claude was buried in the parish cemetery of Notre-Dame-en-Vaux, following a ceremony on 29 July taken by his *beau frère* (brother-in-law) François Huet, *Curé* at Coolus. Claude's sons Jules-Claude-Marie (named as Claude in the Parish record) and Jean-Baptiste were present. Neither Nicolas nor Louis-Gervais was able to return in time for the burial, but they would no doubt have hurried home when the news finally reached them in order to comfort their mother.

It was at this time – in September 1780 – that the very detailed inventory was taken of the Royal Palace Hotel. In addition to the details given above in chapter 1, the list included four employees who lodged at the inn: Jean-Pierre Klein, cook; Marguerite Godfin and Cécile Garlois, domestic servants; and Jérôme Nicaise, waiter.[51]

As an aside, the 1911 eleventh edition of the *Encyclopaedia Britannica* contains an entry on the writer, philanthropist and prison reformer Benjamin Nicolas Appert who was born on 10 September 1797 in Paris. This article states that he was Nicolas's brother (although incorrectly calling him François Appert – an error partially corrected in more recent volumes, which call him Nicolas François Appert).[52] The earliest I can trace this supposed link is to the 1833 *l'Encyclopédie des gens du monde*,[53] which was therefore published while both Benjamin and Nicolas were alive. However, Nicolas's father died in 1780, and his mother, Marie, died in 1790. Even if they had not died, Nicolas's father would have been 86 years old, and his mother 83 at the time of Benjamin's birth!

There is even some confusion over drawings of Appert as a young man – are they of Nicolas or of Benjamin? An example is shown on page 31.

By 1784, as Nicolas was contemplating his next career move, the world was changing. The American colonies had won their independence from England, with the help of the French. France itself was about to be convulsed in major political, military and scientific turmoil. The 1789 revolution and the Terror that followed affected all of France – and much beyond – but it was centred in Paris. It was also to Paris that Nicolas now directed his steps.

Nicolas or Benjamin Appert?

Line drawing by P. de S. Etienne

(From the author's collection)

Nicolas Appert opened his first shop
at *N° 47 rue des Lombards*, Paris

Chapter 3

La Renommée, Paris: 1784 – 1792

Nicolas opened up a confectionery shop at N^o *47 rue des Lombards* in Paris in 1784.[54] Lombard Street is not far to the north of the River Seine and *L'Île de la Cité* (then called *L'Île du Palais*), and midway between the *Palais du Louvre* a mile to the west, and the *place de la Bastille* a mile to the east.

Nicolas named his shop *La Renommée*, meaning the famous or the renowned. He had chosen his street well; this was known to be the confectionery capital of Europe. The *rue des Lombards* is still a busy commercial street. Its houses are tall, with four or five floors above the shop level, now mostly rented or owned as flats. I imagine that Nicolas would have occupied the ground floor, basement and possibly the first floor. He would probably have set up his kitchen behind the shop, and in the basement even from this early stage he is likely to have set up his "laboratory."

On Thursday 14 July 1785 Nicolas, aged 35, married 27 year old Elisabeth Benoist at the church of *Saint Jacques Le Majeur*[55] a short distance away from his shop in Paris. Unfortunately, it is not known how they first met or for how long they had known each other before they married.

Elisabeth had been born in Reims in the parish of St. Peter's on 11 July 1758, the daughter of Jacques-George Benoist and Jeanne Dupuis.[56] Her parents had been shopkeepers in Reims, but then moved to Paris buying a strong glue factory in Corbeil, just south of Paris.

Saint-Jacques Tower, Paris

This is all that remains of *L'église Saint Jacques Le Majeur*

By the time of her marriage, Elisabeth had lost both of her parents. Her father had died on 27 March 1771 at Corbeil-Essonnes. Her mother had then become bankrupt in November 1780, dying a year later on 20 December 1781.[57]

Only the tower remains of the church where Nicolas and Elisabeth married. The church was dedicated to St. James the Greater – *Saint Jacques Le Majeur* – but was more famously known for the butchers' market that surrounded it, and so was called *Saint Jacques La Boucherie*, St. James the Butcher's Shop, or Butchery. From the 11th century the church was the start of the pilgrimage trail along *le Chemin de Saint-Jacques* to another Saint James's Church: Santiago de Compostela in north-west Spain.

Readers of the Harry Potter books might like to know that Nicolas Flamel is said to be buried beneath the stone floor of *Saint Jacques La Boucherie*, as he had endowed the church in 1389; many said that he paid for it with gold from the Philosopher's Stone. Flamel, a bookseller by trade, gave huge sums to the poor and to good causes – including to the *Quinze-Vingts* hospital that comes into Nicolas Appert's story later. Flamel had had the cover stone of his grave in the nave of *Saint Jacques* carved with a sun above a key and a closed book, in the midst of many figures. This and many others of his carvings were studied by those who wanted also to unlock the secrets of the Philosopher's Stone. Given the rumours surrounding Flamel and his wife Pernelle, stories grew up that their deaths and funerals had been staged and that they lived on, secretly. Even if the Flamels did not live on, their house has: it is still standing and is the oldest in the city at about 600 years old, at *Nᵒ 51 rue Montmorency*.

Saint Jacques La Boucherie became the Apperts' parish church, as successive family baptisms testify, until it was destroyed with Revolutionary fervour in 1793   just eight years after the Apperts' wedding. In 1797 the site was auctioned and its stone used for building, with the exception of the tower which was to be kept, although its bells were sold off to a foundry.

Above: Two commemorative roads near *Saint-Jacques* Tower: the *rue Nicolas Flamel* and the *rue Pernelle*

Nicolas and Pernelle Flamel's house
N° 51 rue Montmorency

In 1786 the Appert family moved a few doors down the *rue des Lombards* to number 57.[58] Then on 27 May that year their first child was born: Charles-Pierre-Nicolas.[59] The baptism took place at *L'église Saint Jacques La Boucherie*, with Elisabeth's uncle Pierre Dupuis, King's Counsellor, being his godfather.

Fifteen months later, on 10 August 1787, their first daughter was born: Elisabeth-Marie-Nicole, named after her mother and her grandmother.[60] Her godfather was also from her mother's family – Nicolas Benoist Godinot, a well-to-do Parisian.

On 5 January 1789 Aglaë-Françoise, their second daughter, was born.[61] With three children below three years of age and a shop to run it must have been a busy life.

The winter of 1788 – 1789 was an exceptionally severe one. Snow fell almost daily from New Year's Eve until mid-April. The River Seine froze over; trade of all sorts was virtually impossible; the prices of bread, meat and other goods rose sharply. Many sheep and cattle died in the freezing temperatures. Even messengers on horseback froze to death riding from Paris to Versailles. The harsh reality of hunger and despair that swept France was the prelude to a revolutionary year.

The government, led by finance minister Loménie de Brienne, was facing a deficit in excess of 150 million *livres*. Up and down the country it was proving impossible to collect the *taille*, the taxes. In July 1788, Brienne had persuaded King Louis XVI to take the major step of ordering the recall of the Estates General, for the first time in 175 years, in order to deal with the joint crisis of this financial bankruptcy and the dreadful state of the country.

The Estates General represented the three estates of the realm: church, nobility and commons. The First Estate numbered 10,000 Catholic clergy who owned or administered nearly 10% of the land. The Second Estate, the nobility, comprised about 400,000 people. It was from their number that virtually all positions of rank and authority were filled in the service of the government, army and church. Neither the First nor the Second Estate had to pay tax. Almost the entire tax burden fell on the much more numerous, but far less well off, Third Estate – the commons. At the time of the Revolution 97% of the population of France fell into this category - about 25 million farmers, peasants, and middle class workers.

The three estates were represented by equal numbers of voters in the Estates General. As a result of loud demands, the Third Estate were granted twice as many representatives as each of the other Estates. However, this made no difference to their position, as the Estates retained equal status in terms of their voting power. The representatives of the Third Estate could expect to continue to be outvoted by the combination of the other two Estates.

For the election of representatives of the Third Estate Paris was divided into 60 districts. Nicolas Appert, resident in Lombard Street, was in the Saint Denis neighbourhood of the district of Saint Nicolas in the Fields. In Paris, the qualifications to be a voter were to be a male of at least 25 years of age, having paid annual tax of at least six *livres*. This effectively disenfranchised at least a quarter of male residents, not to mention the entire female population. At the voting on 21 April 1789, Nicolas Appert was one of 343 voters resident in his district who fulfilled these qualifications.[62]

The terrible weather abated in April, but the drastic shortages continued. Tempers flared up at the least rumour, and when it was said that one of the major employers in the *faubourg Saint-Antoine,* the wall-paper manufacturer M. Jean-Baptiste Réveillon, was to cut his workers' wages, there was a riot. This took place on 28 April 1789 and led to his mansion being completely destroyed and anything up to 900 people losing their lives as a result of armed troops firing on the rioters. The rumour turned out to be false – in fact Réveillon was one of the best employers of his time – and thankfully he and his family escaped by climbing a wall and fleeing to the Bastille.

Nicolas was not in Paris on that day. He would have been travelling as, on the following day 29 April 1789, he was back in Châlons. Together with his mother and three brothers, he completed the sale of his birthplace: the White Horse Inn, in the *place Saint Jean*.[63] Marie-Nicolle, Nicolas's mother, was coming up to her 75th birthday and she wanted to sort out the family finances so that everything would be settled and agreed about her estate when she died.

The Estates General convened on Tuesday 5 May 1789, with Louis XVI unsuccessfully attempting to keep tax as the sole item of business. The three Estates instead immediately began to debate the organisation of the legislature.

Meanwhile, Nicolas was back again in Châlons three weeks after his previous visit, on 19 May 1789, to listen to the valuation of the various properties and rents owned by the widow Appert. Nicolas, Louis-Gervais, Jules-Claude-Marie and Jean-Baptiste joined their mother at the Royal Palace Hotel to hear Master Rémy, the notary, list and value everything.

The estate included:

L'Hôtel du Palais Royal	43,000 *livres*
House in the Bell cul-de-sac	8,000 *livres*
Land at Coolus	19,000 *livres*
Rent/other revenue	7,400 *livres*

The total came to about 77,400 *livres*. They then deducted debts, expenses and payments, to achieve a new total of

59,840 *livres*. Each of the four sons would inherit 14,960 *livres*. Nicolas received as his share the house in the Bell cul-de-sac and the 7,400 *livres* from rent and other revenue.[64]

Three days later, Nicolas was back in Paris with Jean-Baptiste, his younger brother. Jean-Baptiste probably met Elisabeth's younger sister Nicole-Sophie Benoist when visiting Nicolas and Elisabeth in Paris sometime earlier. Nicole-Sophie was five years younger than Elisabeth, having been born in Reims in 1763. On Friday 22 May 1789, Jean-Baptiste and Nicole-Sophie were married.[65] After their marriage they travelled back to Châlons, where Nicole-Sophie joined Jean-Baptiste in continuing to run the Royal Palace Hotel with the widow Appert, and then in their own right after Marie-Nicolle's death the following year.

On 4 June 1789 the Dauphin died of tuberculosis. Marie Antoinette and Louis XVI had finally had children following the belated consummation of their marriage in 1773, three years after their wedding. Their second child, and first son, Louis-Joseph-Xavier-François, the Dauphin, had been born on 22 October 1781. He was always a sickly child, though all testified to his pleasant nature. At a time when the King was virtually bankrupt and prices were at the highest anyone had known, 600,000 *livres* was spent on the royal funeral. The death of his son was such a blow to the King that understandably he conducted business without interest over the coming days. He was allowed no time for his private grief by the body of representatives of the Third Estate, however, by now calling itself the Commons.

Then the Commons formed itself on 17 June 1789 into the National Assembly at Versailles under the presidency of Jean–Sylvain Bailly, an astronomer who had calculated the orbit of Halley's Comet and written of the motion of Jupiter's moons. The Commons considered themselves the only properly constituted assembly and immediately declared all current taxes illegal. They called for members of the other two Estates to join them to create a single assembly.

On Saturday 20 June, the Commons were barred from their meeting place, whether by design or owing to the carpenters constructing a large dais for the King, and so the six hundred representatives moved in the heavy rain to a real tennis court, a large hall, nearby in the *rue de Vieux*, and took the Tennis Court Oath "to God and the *Patrie* never to be separated until we have formed a solid and equitable Constitution as our constituents have asked us to."

The National Assembly became the Constituent National Assembly with power to make laws on 9 July. On 11 July Louis XVI decided to dismiss his Director-General of Finance Jacques Necker, believing him to be an encourager of the Commons to revolt against him.

Meanwhile the King garrisoned Versailles and Paris with a large number of soldiers, most of whom were either German or Swiss. Although his stated aim was to keep the peace it was generally believed it was to ensure he kept power. Troops were ordered to clear the mob from the *place Louis XV* (soon to be renamed *place de la Révolution*), but this only succeeded in inflaming the situation. As the troops attempted to withdraw, the *Gardes Françaises* confronted them. This latter force had rebelled against their officers and had turned from being those obeying orders to confront and stop the mob, to being an active part of them.

The royal troops evacuated the area, leaving anarchy behind in the city. At 11pm on Sunday 12 July a meeting of elected representatives at the *Hôtel de Ville* summoned emergency sessions at the sixty district headquarters throughout Paris, to be held the next day. These meetings formed a militia in each district made from those entitled to be electors, both to keep the peace and to face any threat from the King's troops. The total number of civilian troops this put onto the streets of Paris was in the region of 13,000 out of the city's total population of 600,000.

Nicolas was among those who signed up in his district as part of the Lombard militia.[66] The militia was mostly composed of the better off members of the merchant class and of the middle class, since they had to be on duty for one day in every four. Most Parisians could not afford to give so much time away from earning their living.

The militia did not have uniforms or weapons. In order to recognise each other in any conflict, the militia wore the red and blue of Paris as a cockade in their hats. Weapons were more difficult to find: there was, however, a large store at the *Invalides*. On Monday 13 July negotiation was attempted in order to gain access to the weapons, but the authorities tried to stop them. Inevitably it was a crowd – some thought about eighty thousand strong – who invaded *L'Hôtel des Invalides*, where over 30,000 rifles were stored, but with little or no ammunition. It was well known that the powder and ammunition was stored at the Bastille.

The Lombard district named Nicolas Appert as one of its representatives to go to ask for a share of the weapons for the defence of the Section. Nicolas patrolled the Lombard area of Paris throughout the night of 13/14 July, and on into the overcast and grey day.[67]

The Bastille was a fortress and a prison, originally built in the fourteenth century. With walls up to fifteen feet thick and eighty feet high and with eight round towers, it was originally a defence against the English. Conditions depended on the status of the prisoner. The aristocratic prisoners were held in the middle levels of the towers in octagonal rooms some 16 feet in diameter. They were allowed comforts from home and were fed tolerably well.

The fortress was manned by 82 *invalides* pensioners, reinforced by 32 Swiss soldiers. They had two days' supply of food and no water supply. On this day in July, the prison itself contained only seven prisoners. Four were forgers; two lunatics: one an Irishman who sometimes thought he was God and at other times Julius Caesar, and who strangely was thought to be a spy; the second lunatic was suspected of being involved in a plot to assassinate the King; and an aristocrat, the *comte de Solages*, whose family had had him committed on a charge of incest.

On Tuesday 14 July 1789, the Apperts' fourth wedding anniversary, the Parisian mob stormed the Bastille. Initially there were fewer than a thousand laying siege to the fortress, but the number swelled during the day. In spite of all the fighting that took place only eighty-three of the citizens were killed, with another fifteen dying later of their wounds. Only one *invalide* died in the assault. At 5pm the governor surrendered. Many more of the defenders were then killed by the angry mob as they stormed into the Bastille.

Bernard-Réné de Launay was the governor of the prison. He was the son of the previous governor and had actually been born in the Bastille. He was gruesomely murdered by the mob. Then an unemployed cook by the name of Desnot cut off de Launay's head using a pocket knife. The head was carried round the streets of Paris to great applause.

954 of those who were involved in the assault were named *Vainqueurs de la Bastille*. They were awarded a medal or a pension, and a certificate which described their involvement in the triumph. About 70% of them were from the immediate area, the *faubourg Saint-Antoine*, employed as cobblers, cabinet-makers, masons, merchants and tailors. Almost 10% were soldiers who had left their units to join in. Just one was a woman, Marie Haucerne, née Charpentier, a laundress, who received a pension in reward. The youngest I can find is Jean Jacques who was aged 10, although Christopher Hibbert in his book *The French Revolution*[68] said that the

youngest was an 8 year old. However, not all the *Vainqueurs* were given dates of birth in the French National Archive.[69]

The Storming of the Bastille
Tuesday 14 July 1789

Painting by Jean-Pierre-Louis-Laurent Houel (1735 – 1813)[70]

The mob expected a reaction and started to barricade streets. Louis XVI, realising his weak position, agreed to recall Necker. Paris remained in great disorder and ferment. The uncertainty and disarray spread out into the country, which was gripped by the Great Fear that the nobles would destroy the new harvest. Following the adage that the best form of defence is offence, the peasantry sacked the houses of the aristocracy. On 4 August the Constituent National Assembly abolished feudalism.

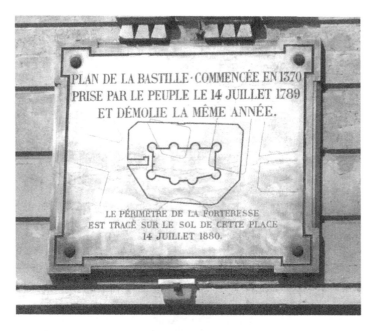

PLAN DE LA BASTILLE·COMMENCÉE EN 1370
PRISE PAR LE PEUPLE LE 14 JUILLET 1789
ET DÉMOLIE LA MÊME ANNÉE.

LE PÉRIMÈTRE DE LA FORTERESSE
EST TRACÉ SUR LE SOL DE CETTE PLACE
14 JUILLET 1880.

Plaque marking the Fall of the Bastille

Place de la Bastille, Paris

In August 1789, the National Guard was being formed in 60 battalions. Nicolas Appert was the first to enrol in his battalion, and began to carry out his guard duties.[71]

On 26 August 1789, the Constituent National Assembly passed "The Declaration of the Rights of Man and of the Citizen." It took until 1946 for women to receive the same rights as men in France.

In the midst of such turmoil, somehow normal life continued. Nicolas visited Châlons again from Wednesday 16 to Monday 21 September in order to continue the arrangements for the disposal of his mother's estate in the event of her death.[72]

La place de la Bastille, Paris

The "July Column" now stands on the site of the Bastille Prison,
commemorating the July 1830 Revolution

King Louis and his family were forcibly relocated from the Palace at Versailles in early October 1789 by a combination of a huge crowd of market-women, or fishwives, many of whom were men dressed as women, and around 20,000 National Guardsmen led by a reluctant Marquis de Lafayette. The cry was for the King to reside in his capital, and so the royal family moved into the Tuileries Palace. The King was now restricted in his movements, a prisoner in all but name, and followed everywhere by six National Guardsmen. The King put it well: "It is wonderful that with such love of liberty on all sides, I am the only person that is deemed totally unworthy of enjoying it."

On Saturday 16 January 1790, Nicolas's mother Marie-Nicolle passed away, aged 75.[73] Exactly a month later, Nicolas was in Châlons to arrange the sale of the house in the Bell cul-de-sac that was part of his inheritance.[74] He received the 8,000 *livres* that it had been valued at: 5,000 immediately and the balance over ten years. Since his wife, Elisabeth, had not been able to go with him to Châlons, the sale had to be ratified in front of a notary on 16 April in their house in *rue des Lombards*.[75]

Nicolas continued to be an active citizen in the Lombard Section, joining in the assembly meetings in *L'église de Saint-Jacques La Boucherie*. There were about 2,500 active citizens in the Section. Active citizens were those who fulfilled the following criteria:

- to be French, or have become French;
- to be at least 25 years old;
- to have been resident in the area for at least a year;
- to have donated the value of at least 3 days' labour;
- not to be in domestic service.

Nicolas rose through the ranks of importance in the Lombard Assembly. At various times he was: the Editorial Representative, conveying the speeches of the National

Convention; Representative in charge of Clothing and Equipment for the Section's volunteers; Representative to the War Committee; Secretary and, by 1793, President of the Lombard Assembly.[76]

The Revolution was always in need of money. In 1790, Citizen Appert paid, out of patriotic duty, 100 *livres*. In May 1792, a further gift of 602 *livres* followed.[77]

La Renommée prospered throughout this time. Although initially simply a confectionery shop, Nicolas developed the shop into a grocery store and began to move towards wholesale trading. He sent goods as far as Rouen and even Marseille, employing a small staff.[78]

The first anniversary of the fall of the Bastille was celebrated on Wednesday 14 July 1790 with the great celebration of the *Fête de la Fédération* on the *Champ de Mars*, the present day site of the Eiffel Tower. Even the tremendous rain failed to dampen the enthusiasm of the crowds. Estimates of the number of people present place it in the region of 500,000. No doubt Nicolas was there as a National Guardsman, taking his turn in the march past of all 83 *départements* following behind their banners.

With *Vainqueurs de la Bastille* in seats of honour, the King and Queen sat through the whole day. At half past three, mass was said by Charles-Maurice de Talleyrand-Périgord, the Bishop of Autun. Talleyrand had earlier been one of the committee that had drawn up the Declaration of the Rights of Man and the Citizen.

The *Fête* was a huge success, culminating in cries of *Vive le Roi!* and *Vive la Reine!* Even the rain stopped and the sun came out, as if to suggest that the future was to be pleasant and hopeful for the monarchy.

However, things did not improve for the King. There was great unrest caused by the Civil Constitution of the Clergy, a measure proposed by Talleyrand, which sought to sever the church from Rome and in effect nationalise it. The Pope,

Pius VI, condemned the move, and formally suspended all priests who accepted the Constitution. The King, who had reluctantly accepted the Constitution, now would not have anything to do with the priests who had accepted it. The people demonstrated against what they saw as the Pope's interference in their affairs. The King was accused of being a traitor, flouting the laws of France by receiving communion from a non-juror priest – one who held to his allegiance to Rome and not France.

On Monday 20 June 1791, attempting to flee the country in disguise and with forged passports, Louis XVI and Marie Antoinette were unlucky to be caught at Varennes. The escape had been very well planned and carried out with the help of Count Fersen, the King of Sweden's special representative to the French court, and a close friend especially of the Queen. Due, however, to the slow progress of the heavily laden *berline* carriage they were travelling in, arrangements for meeting loyal troops along the way fell through.

In the slow procession back to Paris, they stopped the first night at Châlons. This was twenty-one years after Marie Antoinette had first been there en route to meeting Louis, and many must have remembered the celebrations that took place then for it is recorded that many Chalonnais wept for pity. Young girls tried to present the Queen with flowers, but officials from the town prevented them.

Once back in Paris, the King and Queen were from then on prisoners, first in the Tuileries Palace. The Constituent National Assembly suspended the King's authority until 16 July 1791.

The King very reluctantly agreed to the new constitution on 14 September 1791, and the new government – the Legislative Assembly – sat on 1 October. By law, anyone who had sat in the previous Constituent National Assembly was barred from being a member of the Legislative Assembly. The dominant power in this new government was that of the *Girondins*, led by Jacques Pierre Brissot. They believed that it was necessary in order to save the Revolution that France should go to war with the enemies of the Revolution beyond its borders.

Consequently, in April 1792 France declared war on Austria and Prussia, starting the French Revolutionary Wars. The French army, numbering less than 140,000, was disorganised and ill-equipped. It suffered defeat after defeat. Prices started to rise and the mob grew angrier.

In July 1792, possibly in time for the third anniversary celebrations of the fall of the Bastille, Nicolas donated six pikes to his National Guard Section, arming five of his workers and using one himself.[79] The government had recently called for the 48 Sections of Paris (the new number of administrative and representative districts) to admit to their meetings not just the 'active' citizens, as previously, but 'passive' citizens also. They now went further, allowing all citizens who possessed a pike to be a member of the National Guard. This changed the Guard from being a bourgeois body to that of the *sans-culottes*.

The *sans-culottes* were so called because they wore the full-length trousers of the poorer class, as opposed to the silk knee-breeches that were in fashion. Initially therefore the term referred to those volunteers who had little in the way of equipment or clothing, but the term came to mean the working class radicals of the Revolution.

A few months earlier, Roger de Lisle had composed the 'Song of the Rhine Army' when he was stationed at the Strasbourg garrison. The song was picked up in Paris in the early days of August 1792, especially by a group of National Guardsmen from Marseille who had been brought to reinforce Paris. The song has since become known as the *Marseillaise*.

This group of soldiers, together with a large mob, carried out the worst rioting the Revolution had known so far. On Friday 10 August 1792 they attacked the Tuileries Palace. The King and his family only just escaped to take refuge in the nearby Legislative Assembly, while the 900 Swiss Guards and all the servants in the Palace were butchered by the mob.

Nicolas Appert was on Guardsman duty on the streets of Paris that day. The Lombard Section had not been involved in the attack on the Tuileries Palace. Whatever his duties actually were, as a result of his sterling conduct he was promoted on 16 August 1792 to Lieutenant in his company of 126 men, second in rank to his Captain.[80]

The Legislative Assembly decided that Louis and Marie Antoinette, their children and close servants, should be imprisoned in the Temple, initially in the Small Tower. The King was stripped of all titles and honour, becoming Citizen Louis Capet.

The Temple was built in the twelfth century by the Knights Templar as their main headquarters in Europe. By the eighteenth century it had become a fortress and then, in part, a prison. Marie Antoinette was said to have a horror of the Temple prison and had asked her brother-in-law, the *comte d'Artois*, to have it knocked down. It stood until 1808 when Napoleon gave the order to demolish it in order to stop it being a place of pilgrimage.

There was great fear around the city. Each Section had to establish a Vigilance Committee, to look out for counter-revolutionaries and royalists. Hundreds of suspects were imprisoned. In the Assembly Danton called for every man of military age to be drafted into the army to go to the defence of the *Patrie*. The Paris Commune proclaimed "To arms, citizens, to arms, the enemy is at our doors."

Nicolas patriotically donated a further 200 *livres* to his

Section.[81]

The Lombard Section created the 1st Battalion – *le premier bataillon des Lombards* – on 4 September 1792, a volunteer force to join the regular army. Nicolas did not join it himself, but remained in Paris. The next day the Battalion received orders to go to Châlons-sur-Marne, to head towards the Austrian invading army. They arrived there on 12 September.

Meanwhile in Paris the appalling September massacres occurred, when a mob of about 200 toured the prisons night after night from Sunday 2 to Friday 7 September and murdered everyone they could find, regardless of their crime, or suspected offence. The reason behind it, according to those in the Legislative Assembly who should have stopped it but did not, was that when the men went off to fight for their country, they did not want left behind in the city those who would aim to kill their families. So they put them to death to protect their women and children.

There is no doubt that many started to distance themselves from the Revolution at the sight of such excesses.

On 16 September the Army's Commander-in-Chief, Marshall Lükner, ordered the 1st Lombard Battalion to reinforce the army of General Dumouriez. As they made their way to Suippes, about 15 miles north east of Châlons, they were surrounded by the enemy. It was all they could do to escape and return to their base at Châlons.

By Thursday 20 September 1792, the Prussian army, under the Duke of Brunswick, had advanced towards Châlons and faced the large French army at the small village of Valmy.

The 1st Lombard Battalion fought near the Neuville Bridge. Although there were few casualties, this battle was a major turning point in the French Revolutionary Wars. Ten days later the invading army, without firing another shot or engaging the French further, withdrew.

The Battle of Valmy
20 September 1792

Painting by Jean-Baptiste Mauzaisse (1784 – 1844)[82]

This battle, within striking distance of Châlons-sur-Marne, was the second of the "Fifteen Decisive Battles of the World" to take place near Châlons (see page 6).

On this same day, 20 September 1792, the new National Convention met, succeeding the Legislative Assembly. It voted the next day to remove the King from power and to establish a Republic. In October 1793, the National Convention decreed a new calendar, declaring retrospectively that Saturday 22 September 1792 was to become the first day of Year 1 of the new calendar: *1 vendémiaire an I.*

Three months were assigned to each season;
the autumn months were named:

vendémiaire   month of vintage
brumaire   month of fog

frimaire	month of frost

the winter months:

nivôse	month of snow
pluviôse	month of rain
ventôse	month of wind

the spring months:

germinal	month of seeds
floréal	month of blossoms
prairial	month of meadows

and the summer months:

messidor	month of harvesting
thermidor	month of heat
fructidor	month of fruit

The year was divided into 12 months, each of which was 30 days long and was subdivided into three 10-day periods known as *décades*; the last day of each *décade* was a day of rest. The five days remaining at the end of the year (17 to 21 September in the Gregorian calendar) were designated national holidays.

On that first night of the new Republic, at 2am, Nicolas Appert carried out his guard duties, patrolling the *rue de la Boucherie*. The report he later filed at the offices at *N° 207 rue Saint-Martin* shows that he had to deal with at least two rowdy parties that night![83]

12 Franc commemorative stamps
Issued 5 March 1955

Design by Henry Lucien Cheffer (1880 – 1957)

(From the author's collection)

This stamp was one of a collection of six on the theme of
French Inventors. The full list of the six commemorated is:

5F stamp: Philippe Le Bon (1767-1804) – Illuminating Gas
10F: Barthélemy Thimmonier (1793-1859) – Sewing Machine
12F: Nicolas Appert (1749-1841) – Canned Food
18F: Henri Sainte-Claire Deville (1818-1881) - Aluminium
25F: Pierre-Emile Martin (1824-1915) – Steel Making
30F: Hilaire Bernigaud de Chardonnet (1839-1924) - Rayon

Statue to commemorate the 150th anniversary
of Nicolas Appert's death
Châlons-en-Champagne
In bronze by Jean-Robert Ipoustéguy (1920 – 2006)
Erected 1991

Chapter 4

Citizen Appert: From Patriot to Prisoner
1792 – 1795

Nicolas Appert was still living with his wife and three children at *N° 57 rue des Lombards*, Paris, where he ran his wholesale grocery and confectionery business, *La Renommée*. By 1792 he was employing at least six workers and no doubt spending every available moment in his laboratory on his food experiments.[84]

Much of his time was taken up as Lieutenant in the National Guard of the Lombard Section. He attended many meetings and carried out his various duties. Gradually he was becoming more prominent among the community.

Detail from
the front of
the statue shown
opposite

"Nicolas
APPERT
1749 – 1841"

Following the events of the battle of Valmy, Nicolas was involved in an investigation into the conduct of the 1ˢᵗ Lombard Battalion. There had been conflicting reports sent to M. Sevan, the Minister for War, stating either that the 1ˢᵗ Battalion had acquitted themselves well, even taking prisoners of war from an enemy convoy they had met, or that they had fled in cowardly fashion from the convoy and needed rescuing by French Hussars at the cost of the French army losing an advantage.

On 1 October 1792 the Minister for War requested that the President of the Lombard Section look into the matter and establish the facts. A committee of four was set up: the Commander-in-Chief of the Lombard Section army, Citizen Poullent; Commissioner of the army and secretary, Citizen Joly; Citizens Laurent and Appert.

The investigating committee went to rendezvous with the army at Châlons, and from there to view the battlefield. The commissioners interviewed many from the Lombard Battalion and others, including senior officers. The outcome of their enquiry cleared the Battalion's name. The investigating committee had returned to Paris by 11 October.[85]

The *Moniteur Universel* of Tuesday 16 October 1792 reported that the Battalion had been exonerated. It went on to state that General Dumouriez had awarded them, by way of recompense, the position of honour at the next engagement with the enemy.[86] As a result, the 1ˢᵗ Lombard Battalion was in the front line at the Battle of Jemappes on 6 November. Doubtless of the 2,000 French casualties in the French victory that day, there were more than a few from the volunteer 1ˢᵗ Lombard Battalion.

Soon after Nicolas and his colleagues had returned to Paris, the trial of King Louis XVI started. At the beginning of October the King had been separated from his family and installed in the Great Tower of the Temple prison. The rest of the Royal Family followed to the Great Tower, but to a different floor, at the end of the month. The children were allowed to visit their father, until in December Louis was given the choice of the children seeing either him or their mother. Louis saw his children just once again.

On Tuesday 11 December 1792, the National Convention decreed that Louis Capet would be brought before them to answer several charges of treason, culminating in the charge that at the time of the flight to Varennes, Louis aimed to flee the country and return as conqueror.

As the King travelled to and from the National Convention hearings, Nicolas Appert was one of the elected officials who were detailed to accompany the carriage.[87]

The National Convention convicted Louis of high treason by 691 votes against him, a few abstentions, and none voting for him. It took longer to decide the penalty, but finally exile was rejected and a sentence of death was passed on 16 January 1793 by a narrow majority. Louis was told of the sentence at 2pm on Sunday 20 January, with the execution set for the next day. His family were allowed to see him on the Sunday evening.

The Lombard Section chose Nicolas Appert as one of their representatives at the execution of the King,[88] at 11 o'clock on Monday 21 January 1793 in the *place de la Révolution*, previously the *place Louis XV*. Charles Henri Sanson, the hereditary Executioner, operated the guillotine, to the accompanying cheering of the crowd.

At a crucial period of the French Revolutionary Wars, with war being declared on England, Holland and Spain by March 1793, Nicolas became commissioner for the War Committee of the Lombard Section.[89] His responsibilities included overseeing the collection of money for the war effort, maintaining a correspondence with the Battalion at the front, the provision of clothing and equipment for the Battalion, and ensuring that the families of the volunteers were looked after, giving financial and other help where it was needed.

The Execution of "Louis Capet"

From an engraving by Isidore-Stanislas Helman (1743 – 1806)[90]

Nicolas continued to donate not only his time but his material resources, with a donation of a full uniform and of 250 *livres* to the War purse.[91]

Nicolas may also have seen some direct action outside Paris. In March 1793 there was a counter-revolutionary uprising in the *Vendée*, an area in west central France, north of La Rochelle. Tens of thousands of peasants revolted against the revolutionary government, in particular against the Civil Constitution of the Clergy and the imposition of military conscription. It was a ferocious and vicious time, mirroring the worst days in Paris. The National Guard was greatly reinforced from around the country. Nicolas could have been involved in this civil war effort, but no details are known.[92] If he was involved, it would have been for about a month at most, although the troubles continued for three years costing in all around 100,000 lives.

In April 1793, Nicolas was elected President of the General Assembly of the Lombard Section. As such he was one of the leading men of the city, and clearly a renowned Patriot. He corresponded with the National Convention on behalf of his Section.[93]

However, the war was going badly: Britain was besieging Dunkirk; Spain was ready to cross the Pyrenees; Sardinia was about to re-take Savoy; Prussia and Austria had both recently defeated French forces in the east and north. Prices were continuing to rise and unemployment was spiralling. The Convention was in trouble with intense pressure from the Paris mobs of *sans-culottes*. The Convention decreed special criminal tribunals to deal with political prisoners, little knowing that most of those who voted for them would be in front of them before too long.

The Committee of the Twelve then called for the records to be handed in to them of the deliberations of all Paris Sections in order to examine their contents and to look into all arrests made and activities carried out over the last few months.

With the frequent election rules in the Sections, Nicolas was replaced as President in May by his friend Charles-Louis Limodin. Nicolas became Secretary. In response to the decree of the Committee of Public Safety, Limodin and Nicolas delivered the Section's records to them.

Several citizens, including Nicolas, called for a 9am meeting of the Lombard Assembly on Friday 17 May 1793, to discuss the rising tensions in the government. The assembly was summoned, but for 2pm. Some citizens could not attend because of their work.

Things were about to go badly wrong for Nicolas Appert. As the cross-currents of revolution and counter-revolution washed through the streets of Paris, it became a very thin line between being a Patriot or an enemy of the state. Both Nicolas and his friend Charles-Louis Limodin were now dismissed from all of their official positions in the Section. When the General Assembly of the Lombard Section met at the end of May it decided that:

> The citizens Limodin and Appert have taken the record of the deliberations of the Section to the Committee of the Twelve of the National Convention, without having first warned the Assembly.
>
> They will be denounced to the prosecutor of the Commune as having removed the register while being president and secretary of the Section – positions which they no longer hold – and without referring to the Assembly;
>
> They have both been dismissed from their places as Commissioners of the Military Committee, of assessors of Justices of the Peace, and every civilian and military grade conferred by the Section, and, moreover, citizen Limodin will no longer be the Section's printer.[94]

Meanwhile, in the Convention, attention focussed on Brissot and the *Girondins* as scapegoats, with calls growing for their summary arrest. A Paris Insurrection Committee, newly formed, incited the mob to surround and then invade the National Convention, calling for the imprisonment of the Girondin deputies. Finally Danton gave in and the names of 22 leading *Girondins* were read out by Marat in the chamber, declaring their arrest. Nicolas joined in this siege, saying that from 31 May to 2 June he did not put down his weapons. This was Nicolas's last act in support of the Revolution.[95]

Revolt was spreading throughout the provinces and the Convention seemed powerless to act. Danton lost power and Maximilien Robespierre replaced him on 27 July, taking over the leadership of the Committee of Public Safety. The Committee resolved to prosecute enemies of the Revolution, namely all foreigners resident in France, *Girondins*, noble officers in the army, and anyone who could not obtain a certificate of "good citizenship" from the Vigilance Committee of their Section.

Maximilien François Marie Isidore de Robespierre (1758 – 1794)

From an anonymous portrait c1790[96]

On Monday 3 June 1793, Nicolas and his family moved house. While keeping the shop and laboratory at *N° 57 rue des Lombards*, the family moved to the first floor of *N° 178 rue Saint Denis*.[97] This house was in the neighbouring Section of *Les Amis de la Patrie*. The house had an imposing portico front and was near the corner of *rue aux Ours* (Bear Street). Sadly, the house was knocked down to make way for *rue Etienne Marcel* in the 19th century.

The move may already have been planned, but it seems possible that the family moved out of the Lombard Section in order for Nicolas to evade the charges being put up against him with the Section's prosecutor. If this was so, it was not successful because the allegations followed him to his new Section. On Tuesday 4 June Nicolas was summoned to *N° 52 rue Quincampoix* where *Les Amis de la Patrie* Section's Vigilance and Public Safety Committee met.[98]

At that meeting he was asked to surrender his weapons, but told the Committee that he had none. He was also asked whether he had been the author of the petition to convene the Assembly on 17 May at the Lombard Section and whether he had taken the register of the Lombard Section's deliberations and given it to the office of the Committee of the Twelve. He denied both accusations.

Nicolas's case was referred to the General Assembly of the Section for judgement concerning these "offences."

Shortly afterwards, on Friday 28 June 1793, a search of Nicolas's house was authorised.[99] An armed force accompanied two Commissioners of Vigilance, Jacques-François Bellement and Pierre-Louis Cretinier, as they carried out a thorough search of *N° 178 rue Saint Denis*. However, nothing incriminating was discovered. On the contrary, they found several things to confirm Nicolas as a Patriot: receipts for donations made to the Lombard Section and various patriotic printed publications. The Commissioners reported that Elisabeth, showing perhaps more spirit than good sense, had declared to them that she "had no weapons, but that if she did have guns she would not give them up to us, as she does not serve anyone."

On the next day Nicolas went again to *Les Amis de la Patrie* headquarters to pick up his papers as a resident of this new Section. Previously in his papers from the Lombard Section he had declared himself to be *confiseur* or confectioner; now he signed himself as *marchand* or merchant:

Security Card issued by the Revolutionary Committee of the Section of *Les Amis de la Patrie*: No. 2557

Dated:	29 June [1793]
Name	Appert, Nicolas
Profession:	Merchant
Age:	42
Address:	178 *rue Saint-Denis*
Previous Address:	*rue des Lombards*
Arrived in Paris:	1784
Place of Birth:	Châlons

Under Observation

Signed: Appert[100]

On Tuesday 23 July 1793, in the middle of all this turmoil, Elisabeth gave birth to their third daughter Amélie-Justine, born at 1am at home in *rue Saint Denis*.[101] By this time, their children's ages were: Charles-Pierre-Nicolas 7, Elisabeth-Marie-Nicole nearly 6, and Aglaë-Françoise 4. Due to the de-Christianization of Revolutionary France, Amélie-Justine was not baptised, but registered at *Les Amis de la Patrie* Section offices. One of the two witnesses was Nicolas's brother Louis-Gervais Appert, who had moved back from the Netherlands at some time previously and was now a caterer at Rethel, about 40 miles north of Châlons-sur-Marne. At some stage, Louis-Gervais had married Marie Couttin and this may have been the reason for coming back to France.

Unfortunately, although a few quiet weeks passed for Nicolas and Elisabeth, their troubles were not over. On *22 vendémiaire an II* (Sunday 13 October 1793) the order was given for another search. This time, however, it was of Appert's grocery and confectionery shop in Lombard Street. Nicolas was not present at the search. The two commissioners, MM. Delaunay and Dizy, searched the shop, including Nicolas's laboratory, but left without finding anything against Nicolas.[102]

The Reign of Terror was well under way, especially following the passing of the Law of Suspects by the National Convention on 17 September 1793. This created Revolutionary Tribunals that tried those suspected of treason against the Republic, often with very little evidence. It did not take much to be tried and convicted of "crimes against liberty" and the guillotine awaited those found guilty, with no process of appeal.

At 12.15pm on Wednesday 16 October 1793, Marie Antoinette was guillotined at *la place de la Révolution*. Her priest had said to her "This is the moment, Madame, to arm yourself with courage." Marie Antoinette replied with spirit: "Courage! The moment when my ills are going to end is not the moment when courage is going to fail me." She went up to the platform so eagerly that she inadvertently trod on the executioner's foot. Her last words were therefore "Monsieur, I beg your pardon. I did not do it on purpose." The executioner, Henri Sanson, son of Louis's executioner, then carried out his duties.

Later that month the 22 *Girondins* went on trial and were condemned to death. One Parisian said that it had become dangerous to be considered less revolutionary than your neighbour. Louis Antoine Léon de Saint-Just, a close ally of Robespierre, said "We must rule by iron those who cannot be ruled by justice. You must punish not merely traitors, but the indifferent as well." Many were arrested, sentenced and killed on the strength of denunciations by vindictive neighbours; proof and fact were unnecessary complications.

Perhaps it is not too surprising that Nicolas Appert was last heard of in Paris on Thursday 7 November 1793.[103] Since Nicolas needed an internal passport to leave the city, he must have convinced the authorities that it was a business trip – which it probably initially was. However, it was to be six months before his – enforced – return to Paris.

In his absence, *Les Amis de la Patrie* Section Vigilance

Committee made this declaration on *25 brumaire an II* (15 November 1793):

> In discussing suspected men, citizen Appert was considered. He was a dangerous man in the Revolution, always covered by the mask of patriotism. He was a Jacobin in the time when Brissot was in power.
>
> He furtively took the registers of the General Assembly of the Lombard Section (where he then resided) to the Inquisitorial Commission. He was disarmed by that Section.
>
> In consequence, the committee decrees that the above-named is suspect and that he will be arrested...[104]

Four days later, on Tuesday 19 November, Elisabeth was visited by the Commissioner of the Vigilance Committee and his Assistant at her home in the *rue Saint Denis*. She declared that she did not know the whereabouts of her husband. A few weeks later, on *23 frimaire an II* (Friday 13 December 1793), the Vigilance Committee conducted a second search of *N° 178 rue Saint Denis*.[105] Again, nothing of an incriminating nature was found. It is hard not to think that the Committee were just aiming to make life difficult for Elisabeth and her children.

Nicolas's movements at this time are not known, except for the period from *23 frimaire an II* (16 February 1794) until *1 germinal an II* (21 March) for which there is a certificate of residence granted for him by the Commune of Saint-Quentin, about 80 miles north east of Paris, at the home of Renard Virly, *place de la Loi*.[106]

On *25 ventose an II* (14 March 1794), *Les Amis de la Patrie* Section Vigilance Committee wrote to Elisabeth Appert. They now gave an additional reason for her husband to be on their suspected list, namely because of his prolonged absence from Paris. Elisabeth strongly defended her husband in her reply. She wrote that her husband could only have left Paris with a passport issued by the Committee themselves, and that he often left Paris and was absent for a long period of time on business. She stoutly claimed that his commitment to the Republic was far too great for him to seriously consider emigration, as any who knew him well could testify. She told them that there would never be any evidence of wrongdoing found against Nicolas, and that the enemies pursuing her husband must either be deceived and misled on his account, or enemies of true Patriots.[107]

By way of reply, the Committee issued a new ordinance on *23 germinal an II* (12 April 1794), "demanding the arrest of Appert – enemy of the republican regime."

On *29 germinal an II* (Friday 18 April) Nicolas Appert was arrested at *N° 27 rue de l'Arbalète* in Reims. The arresting officers were Commissioners Dardare Père and Lelièvre, who were accompanied by an armed force and a Justice of the Peace named Citizen Gauthier.[108]

The house where Nicolas was caught, in the Revolutionary Section of Reims, was the home of his wife's cousin Nicolas-Louis Benoist. He was the son of Elisabeth Appert's father's brother, Nicolas Benoist, and was a noted Jacobin.

Nicolas Appert was briefly first put under arrest in Reims in *La Belle Tour* prison. He was soon transferred to Paris and incarcerated in the Madelonnettes Prison, at *N° 18 rue des Fontaines*, just about half a mile north-east of *N° 178 rue Saint Denis*.

Conditions in the Madelonnettes were atrocious. The prison had been converted from an old convent, founded in the early 17th century, and was greatly overcrowded with up to 12 prisoners in some cells. The stench was overpowering with little or no ventilation. The smell was strongest from the toilet block at one side of the site, used by all 300 prisoners. The leading actors from the *Comédie Française* were also imprisoned there at the time. On Monday 2 September 1793 they had been performing the stage version of Samuel Richardson's novel "Pamela," adapted by *abbé Prévost.* A member of the audience shouted out an objection to one of the lines in the play, only to be shouted at in turn by the rest of the audience, telling him to be quiet. He went off to denounce the actors to the Jacobin Club. The leading actor, Dazincourt, and 12 other actors were then all arrested and thrown in the Madelonnettes Prison.

No visitors were allowed at the Madelonnettes Prison. It must have been a place without hope. Nicolas had not seen his wife and children since November, and was not to see them until the very end of July/early August. During that nine month period, and especially when in the Madelonnettes, he must have had times when he despaired of ever seeing them again.

The Vigilance Committee of the Lombard Section sent a thorough and complete dossier of accusations against Nicolas to *Les Amis de la Patrie* Section. They wrote:

The said Appert was among the most scheming in the Lombard Section, having acted the Patriot for six months, but the good citizens saw through him and he was reproached in the General Assembly with being a bad Jacobin. He disrupted the assembly at the time Dumouriez betrayed the Republic. He has done what he could to prevent the recruitment of 300,000 men.

He took the assembly register to the Committee of the Twelve, removing it from the Civil Committee when the secretary was absent, in complicity with Limodin, who is also detained.

He has accused Patriots of the tactic of removing honest people to replace them with riff-raff during the purge of the Commune in 1793.

He sought signatures to convoke an assembly at 2pm, an hour at which the Patriots are at their work, which is nothing less than ordering the death of liberty.

He intrigued at the time of great disturbances to get himself named president.[109]

Madelonnettes Prison, Paris

from a painting by
Louis Léopold Boilly (1761 – 1845)[110]

On Sunday 4 May 1794, Elisabeth Appert wrote to *Les Amis de la Patrie* Vigilance Committee. Instead of pleading for Nicolas's release, she tried a different approach. The business was suffering because Nicolas was in prison and because the Section had taken the business papers into their possession. The goods in the shop had also been impounded.

On *29 floréal an II (*18 May 1794), Nicolas wrote from prison:

To the General Security Committee of the People's Representatives of the National Convention:
I have devoted myself with great zeal to the Revolutionary cause... *[He then describes his actions in support of the Revolution from its beginning until the point of the accusations*

against him in June 1793] But since slander weighs on me, I am forced to give you proof that I have faithfully served my country with all my abilities…

Nicolas then listed all the donations he had made to the cause and he assured them that he had carried out no wrong doing. He continued:

Based on my clear conscience and true principles from which I have never deviated, I wait with great certainty for the wonderful day when my innocence will overcome imposture and slander… You give justice to the oppressed republicans; you destroy the enemies of *La Patrie*… Reunite two virtuous spouses, return a father to the family for whom he is the only means of support, and grant freedom to an old and true Patriot.[111]

Several other letters followed, all with the same negative result. Nicolas was never brought before the Revolutionary Tribunal to answer charges. He was simply left where he was in the Madelonnettes Prison. On *7 messidor an II* (Wednesday 25 June 1794) Elisabeth tried again:

Incorruptible Republican,

I take the liberty of writing a summary of the revolutionary and political life of my husband. I ask you in the name of *La Patrie* and of liberty to read it. It is as a mother of four children that I ask on behalf of my husband: a father of a family, a Patriot of 1789 …[112]

Nothing seemed able to provoke a response. The powerlessness of their position must have been difficult to bear, as well as the uncertainty, the separation and the potential for an arbitrary judgement to fall without notice, swiftly as a guillotine blade.

In the end it was the events of *9 thermidor an II* (Sunday 27 July 1794) that broke the deadlock. Robespierre was overthrown, being guillotined without trial the next day. The newspaper headlines declared "The tyrant is no more" – the Terror was over.

The Thermidorian Reaction to the Terror led to the release of many political prisoners – including the 300 packed into the Madelonnettes. Before long, after about four months of imprisonment, Nicolas was home in *rue Saint Denis*, reunited with his family. He had not seen Amélie-Justine, now just past her 1st birthday, since she was three months old.

It is easy to imagine someone of Nicolas's energies throwing himself straight back into his work, both in his wholesale business and in his researches. By December he was looking to leave Paris for his first business trip. He applied for an interior passport dated *22 frimaire an III*, (Friday 12 December 1794).[113] This was to allow him to journey on business to Saint-Quentin. He then went to Reims, probably to meet up with Elisabeth's family, arriving on *6 nivôse an III* (Friday 26 December 1794).

This interior passport contains a physical description of Nicolas:

> Citizens, permit Nicolas Appert, merchant, to pass... residing at N° 178 St. Denis Street, travelling to the district of Saint-Quentin in the Department of Aisne.
>
> Aged 45 years, height 5 feet 2 inches, chestnut hair and eyebrows, blue eyes, short nose and thin lips, average cleft chin, clear forehead, oval and marked face.
>
> He states the intention to follow the road to Saint-Quentin. If he deviates, place him under arrest. Completed at the Civil Committee of the Section of *Les Amis de la Patrie* on *22 frimaire an III* of the French Republic and the said Appert has signed with us.

The only other description I have found of Nicolas comes from an 1889 French Government Report (*Rapports du Jury sur L'Exposition Universelle Internationale de 1889*) which contains a short biography of Nicolas. It says of him: "The very few people who knew him remember a small man, cheerful, hard-working, helpful, kind and always on the go."[114] This is a description from his time at Massy, around 1810.

As late as February 1795 Nicolas had not yet recovered all the business papers that had been taken in the searches of his premises. He asked for them at *Les Amis de la Patrie* Section offices on *5 ventôse an III* (23 February 1795), and finally received everything back eleven days later.[115]

With the events of his time avoiding arrest and his imprisonment behind him, Nicolas was back to normal. Family life, however, rarely stands still for long. On Wednesday 15 April 1795, Nicolas and Elisabeth's fifth child – and fourth daughter – was born. They named her Angélique-Eloïse. In spite of all the de-Christianization throughout the Revolution since 1789, she was baptised, on Saturday 18 April at the Oratory in the Church *Notre Dame de Blancs Manteaux* in Paris, just over half a mile from where they lived.[116] Their family was now complete.

A new phase of Nicolas's life and career was about to begin. As previously, it was signified by a move. This time, eleven years after opening *La Renommée*, and having lived there and then at two other nearby addresses, the family made a break with Paris and moved about 5 miles south-east to the village of Ivry.

Commemorative First Day Cover Postcard
5 March 1955

(From the author's collection)

Chapter 5

Ivry: The Breakthrough 1795 – 1802

Now a large suburb of Paris, Ivry-sur-Seine was in the late 18th century a small village of about 900 people, situated a short distance outside the Parisian walls through *la barrière Gobelins*, the Gobelin Gate, in the *faubourg Saint-Marcel*. The Gate was named after the *Manufacture des Gobelins*, a tapestry factory that is still on the same site today.

In May or June 1795, the Appert family moved into a house near the *place Frambour* (or *Frambourg*) less than half a mile from the centre of the commune of Ivry.[117]

Commemorating Nicolas Appert in Ivry:
Résidence Nicolas Appert,
at *N° 81 – 85 rue Marat, Ivry-sur-Seine*
– accommodation for 207 students, built in 2004

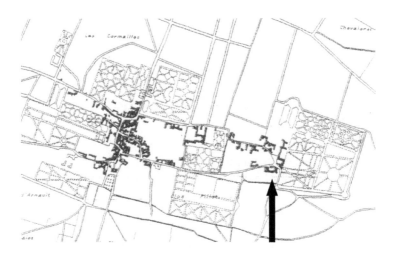

From a 1765 plan of Ivry-sur-Seine
The Apperts lived near the *place Frambour(g)*,
now renamed *place Parmentier*,
which is in the cluster of buildings
to the right of the plan, indicated by the arrow[118]

The Apperts' new house no doubt provided more space for the family of five children, all of whom were under 10 years of age: Charles-Pierre-Nicolas aged 9, Elisabeth-Marie-Nicole 8, Aglaë-Françoise 6, Amélie-Justine 2, and Angélique-Eloïse just a few weeks old.

Nicolas had borrowed the large sum of 3,000 *livres* from his younger brother Jean-Baptiste in April 1795 in order to be able to afford the move.[119] Jean-Baptiste and his wife Nicole-Sophie (Elisabeth's sister) were at this time the owners of the Royal Palace Hotel, and having to change the hotel name frequently to keep the revolutionary spirits in Châlons-sur-Marne happy, as mentioned above in the first chapter.

Nicolas soon became a leading community figure in their new commune. Within at most a few weeks of moving into their new house, at 6pm on *11 messidor an III* (Monday 29 June 1795), Nicolas attended a meeting of the Municipal Council of Ivry, and was elected to be one of the five *Officiers Municipaux*. At the time, Ivry did not have a town hall and so meetings took place in one of the Council members' houses.

In the Municipal Archives of Ivry-sur-Seine for *11 messidor an III* there is the following record:

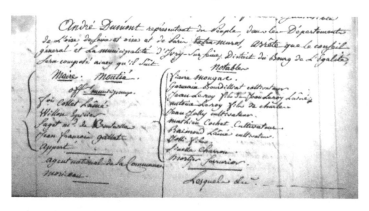

André Dumont, People's Representative in the Departments of Oise, Seine-et-Oise, and Paris (outside the walls), declares that the General Council of the Municipality of Ivry, District of *Bourg de l'Égalité*, will from now on be composed of:

Mayor: Moutié

Municipal Officers: François Collet the Elder
Willon, grocer
Saget, bottle manufacturer
Jean-François Gallet
Appert[120]

However, Nicolas protested that, as he had not lived in Ivry long, others should have the honour above him. The meeting consequently appointed him as Municipal Officer, pending the decision of the area official.

As part of Nicolas's protest at the honour being awarded him by the commune, he gave as a second reason that he could only see with difficulty. Although spectacles were available by the early 19th century, and had been for quite some time, the French were extremely self-conscious about wearing them and it is likely that Nicolas simply did not seriously consider having either a single lens or a pair of spectacles to help overcome the problem. The most famous example of a short-sighted Frenchman of this era who likewise never wore spectacles was the erstwhile Louis XVI. Marie Antoinette's lady-in-waiting, the *Comtesse de La Tour du Pin*, wrote: "He was so short-sighted that he could not recognise anyone at a distance of more than three paces."

Nicolas continued as provisional Municipal Officer from *11 messidor* to *23 thermidor an III* (29 June to 10 August 1795), at which point the appointment was confirmed by the agreement of the district's *procureur syndic*. During those seven weeks he attended 13 meetings of the Council. Records show that he rarely missed a meeting thereafter.[121]

Signatures at the end of the record of the meeting of the
*Municipalité et du conseil general
de la commune D'Ivry Sur Seine
11 messidor an III de la République française*
with Appert's signature in the centre[122]

In this role in the Municipal Council, Nicolas was one of the commune's recorders of births, marriages and deaths, and also a signatory on interior passports. His first official act was six days after his provisional appointment, on *17 messidor an III* (5 July 1795). In Nicolas's handwriting, the record states:

> Today *17 messidor* of the third year of the French Republic ... at four pm – before me Nicolas Appert Municipal Officer of the commune of *Ivry sur Seine* in *L'Egalité* District in the *Département* of Paris... declared that Françoise-Victoire Leroux aged 13 days died today at 4 am... [123]

Nicolas Appert's handwriting and signature
from part of the above entry

At the same time as the entry recording the death of Françoise-Victoire Leroux, Appert wrote an entry in the Births section of the record that Marie-Thérèse, daughter of gardener Jean-Baptiste Legrand and wife Marie Anne, was born the previous day. [124]

On the Municipal Council with him was Jean-André Saget, a bottle and glassware manufacturer. Born in Metz in 1759, Saget had opened a glassware factory in Ivry in 1792. From about this time, Nicolas bought his bottles for his preserving process from Saget's works. There is a later record for example of an order for 8,500 *francs* dated 22 December 1803 for large-necked bottles to be supplied to the Appert factory in Massy.[125]

Nicolas had been carrying out his research into ways of preserving foodstuffs since around 1790, during the early days of the Revolution, when he ran his shop in the *rue des Lombards*. This can be inferred from a statement, he wrote in his best-selling book of 1810 entitled "The Book For All Households, or The Art of Preserving All Kinds of Animal and Vegetable Substances for Several Years":

> My problem is: to preserve all nutritive substances with all their peculiar and constituent qualities. My experiments prove that I have resolved this problem.
>
> It is to the solution of this problem that I have devoted my fortune and twenty years of labour and meditation. Happy that I have already been able to render service to my fellow citizens and humanity, I rely on the justice, generosity and intelligence of a wise government, which never fails to encourage useful discoveries...[126]

Nicolas's starting point was to find a completely different way of approaching the problem of preserving food. In his book, he neatly sums up previous methods in his first paragraph:

> All the imaginable means heretofore used for preserving foods or medicines are reduced to two principal methods; one in which desiccation is employed, the other in which more or less of a characteristic foreign substance is added to prevent fermentation and putrefaction. It is in following the first of

these methods that dried fruits and vegetables, smoked meats, and salted fish are obtained. By the second are obtained fruits and different parts of vegetables preserved in sugar; juices and decoctions of plants reduced to syrups or in extracts; vegetables, fruits, and buds preserved in vinegar; meats, herbs, and vegetables salted; but all those means carry more or less objection. Drying destroys the aroma, changes the flavour of the juices, and shrivels the fibrous tissue or parenchyma. Whatever may be the savour, even in those which are very sapid, the sugar masks and destroys in part other savours, the presence of which it is desired to preserve, such as the agreeable acidity of many fruits. A second objection is that a great deal of sugar is required in order to preserve a small quantity of any other vegetable matter, and upon this account it is not only very costly but also detrimental in some cases. [127]

Nicolas developed in his laboratory the equipment and the methods to solve this problem. He seems to have achieved something of a breakthrough before 1800, when in Ivry, for he speaks of success for more than a ten year span in his 1810 book:

This method is not a vain theory. It is the fruit of reflection, investigation, long attention and numerous experiments, the results of which, for more than ten years, have been so surprising, that notwithstanding the proof acquired by repeated practice, that provisions may be preserved for two, three and six years, there are many persons who still refuse to credit the fact. [128]

In fact, he almost certainly made the breakthrough with his discovery in 1795, the year he moved to Ivry. This can be deduced from two statements Nicolas made. He wrote in 1811:

Over the last 16 years a new branch of business in preserved food substances has been created by this method. [129]

In 1810 Nicolas wrote that, using his preservation methods:

> In this way my family has been, for the space of fifteen years, in the habit of making use of currant juice.[130]

His success generated the growth of his wholesale business. He could supply both local and distant markets with food that would be as fresh when opened as when it was bottled, and with the same flavour and odour. The basis of this success was heat. He developed a series of procedures to ensure that the bottle was of sufficient quality, that the corking created a proper seal and that the timing of boiling was correct. Nicolas wrote in 1810:

> I owe to my experiments and above all to a great perseverance, the conviction, first, that the subject of heat has the essential quality in itself not only of changing the combination of the constituent parts of animal and vegetable products, but also that, if not destroying, at least of arresting for many years the natural tendency of these same products to decomposition; second, that its application in a proper manner to all these products, after having deprived them in the most rigorous manner possible of contact with the air, effects perfect preservation of these same products with all their natural qualities.
>
> Before entering into the details of the execution of my process, I ought to say that it consists principally:
>
> 1st To enclose in the bottle or jar the substances that one wishes to preserve;
>
> 2nd To cork these different vessels with the greatest care because success depends chiefly on the closing;
>
> 3rd To submit these substances thus enclosed to the action of boiling water in a water-bath for more or less time according to their nature and in the manner that I shall indicate for each kind of food;
>
> 4th To remove the bottles from the water-bath at the time prescribed.[131]

NICOLAS APPERT
(1749-1841)
Inventeur du procédé de conservation des Aliments

Commemorative First Day Cover Postcard
5 March 1955

(From the author's collection)

More details of the process that Nicolas developed will be described in the next chapter when we reach his factory at Massy.

On *4 frimaire an VI* (24 November 1797), Nicolas became *adjoint municipal,* a Municipal Assistant, effectively the Mayor's deputy. He continued in this role until *12 ventose an VII* (1 March 1799). Nicolas then became *conseiller municipal,* a Municipal Councillor. [132]

He became Secretary of the Assembly from *15 pluviose an* X (4 February 1802) to *19 floréal an X* (9 May 1802). He did not hold this post long as the family moved to Massy later that year.

Nicolas moved from his shop at 57 Lombard Street during his time at Ivry. In a footnote in the 1831 4th edition of his book, Nicolas wrote that "the author was for fifteen years a confectioner in Lombard Street, Paris,"[133] Since Nicolas set up *La Renommée* in Lombard Street in 1784, this would imply a move in 1799.

The business did not move far – just about 300m to N^o *402 rue Neuve-Saint-Merry.*[134] This road, now called *rue Saint-Merry,* was just to the east of Lombard Street in the neighbouring *Section de la Réunion.* The shop was owned by grocer Nicolas Valentin Cailliet and so Nicolas would have rented the premises. There is an entry in the French National Archives for *22 pluviôse an X* (11 February 1802) for an inventory of *N° 402 rue Neuve-Saint-Merry* following Cailliet's death.[135] Nicolas may have purchased the shop at that point, or possibly continued to rent it from the new owners.

Meanwhile, Nicolas was also on the lookout to move his family again. His aim was to increase his capacity to produce his preserved foods and so his design was to open and equip a factory.

Envelope franking showing
Appert and his factory at Massy
Dated 5 January 1984

(From the author's collection)

Le Château d'en Haut, Massy

The address is now *N° 18 rue Gabriel Péri*,
home to the *Centre Saint-Éxupéry*

Chapter 6

Massy: From the "Chateau on High" to a Financial Low 1802 – 1806

While Nicolas and family were at Ivry, the Revolution had come to an end. On *18 brumaire an VII* (8 November 1799) Napoleon, with support pre-eminently from Talleyrand, had staged the coup that eventually removed the Directorate and set up a Consulate of three, with Napoleon himself soon becoming First Consul.

Although the French Revolutionary Wars continued until the Treaty of Amiens in March 1802, the fighting was mostly outside France: in places such as Austria, Switzerland, Germany, Italy, Denmark and Egypt. However, the British Navy conducted an effective blockade of France – which had an effect on Nicolas's fortunes as we shall see.

The peace lasted a little over a year until war broke out again between Britain and France in May 1803.

On 2 December 1804 Napoleon placed a crown on his own head at the *Cathédrale de Notre Dame de Paris* making himself Emperor of the French, subsequently replacing the French Republic with the French Empire. The "Napoleonic Wars," which involved many other nations in various coalitions, lasted until Wellington's victory at Waterloo on Sunday 18 June 1815. Turmoil continued throughout the period that Nicolas Appert was at Massy.

In *brumaire an XI* (November 1802), during the months of peace between the wars, Nicolas bought a large estate in

Massy from a M. Collinet. The place he chose was a large area of about 14 acres (about 5.6 hectares), with an imposing house at its centre: *Le Château d'en Haut.*[136]

Le Château d'en Haut, Massy

From an old postcard "*Massy autrefois*"

(From the author's collection)

The whole area of land Nicolas bought was bounded by *la route de Chartres, la Voie fondue, la Brèche aux Vieux* and *la ruelle des Sablons*. *La Voie fondue* has now been renamed after André Chénier, a contemporary of Nicolas. Chénier was a poet and writer, and an outspoken critic of the Revolution. He was arrested a month earlier than Nicolas was, and was sentenced to death by guillotine. The sentence was carried out just two days before the Thermidor Reaction, when Robespierre was overthrown.

Chapter 6. Massy: From the "Chateau on High" to a Financial Low
1802 – 1806

Section Number	Owner	Type of Property	Area of plot (m²)
365	Appert	house and courtyard	2,240
366	Appert	garden and building	310
367	Appert	garden	400
368	Appert	master house	370
369	Appert	pleasure garden	660
370	Appert	vegetable garden	10,130
371	Appert	land	5,320
372	Appert	land	7,390
373	Appert	land	13,210
374	Appert	vine	1,820
375	Appert	land	14,040

Record of the property bought
by Nicolas Appert in 1802[137]

rue Appert, Massy
Commemorative road name,
opposite the site of the Apperts' house.
There are also two schools (an *École Elémentaire* [Primary
School] and *École Maternelle* [Nursery School]) in Massy
named after Nicolas Appert

Le Château d'en Haut was the main building Nicolas
bought, but there was another substantial house close by,
with a courtyard and gardens. This was where the Appert
family made their home. Unfortunately, this house has not
survived, but on the building currently occupying the site of
this house, there is a plaque and a medallion
commemorating the fact that Nicolas lived there.

The houses were surrounded by a lot of farm land and a
vine. Nicolas cultivated beans, peas and other crops in order
to bottle them in his factory. Before long, in season, Nicolas
employed up to 30 women in shelling peas and beans alone.
The factory came to have a permanent staff of about 50, all
under the personal direction of Nicolas himself. This was the
world's first factory to produce preserved food.

"At the location of this building
stood the house and workshop of

NICOLAS APPERT

Born in 1749 at Châlons-sur-Marne
Died at Massy on 1 June 1841

INVENTOR of the process of food preservation"

Commemorative plaque and medallion

rue Gabriel Péri, Massy

Detail of the commemorative bronze medallion
shown on the previous page.

By Roland Irolla
(1935 –)
rue Gabriel Péri, Massy

Nicolas designed the suite of rooms in the factory to
accommodate the various processes that his preservation
techniques needed. In "The Book For All Households, or
The Art of Preserving All Kinds of Animal and Vegetable
Substances for Several Years," Nicolas describes the
arrangements:

My laboratory consists of four apartments. The first of these is furnished with all kinds of kitchen utensils, stoves and other apparatus, necessary for dressing the animal substances to be preserved, as well as with a kettle for broth, gravy, etc, of capacity 180 French pints, raised on brick work. This kettle is provided with a pot to be put within it, pierced with holes like a skimmer, with divisions for holding various kinds of meat and poultry.

This pot can be put into and taken out of the kettle with ease. The kettle is provided with a wide cock, to which is fitted, within, a little rose, like that of a watering-can, covered with a piece of cloth. In this way I can produce quite clear broth or gravy, which is ready to be put into bottles.

The second apartment is given over to the preparing of milk, cream and whey.

The third is used for corking and tying the bottles and vessels, and putting them into bags.

The fourth is furnished with three large copper boilers, placed upon stones raised on brick work. These boilers are all furnished with a stout lid, fitted, to rest upon the vessels within. Each boiler is furnished with a wide cock below, in order to let out the water at the proper time. These large boilers are destined to receive, generally, all the objects intended to be preserved, in order to apply the action of heat to them in a suitable manner; and thus they constitute so many water-baths.[138]

The third room contained several items of equipment vital to the successful application of his method. Nicolas could not over-emphasise how important adequate corking and sealing was. He specified:

1. Rows of bottle racks round the room.
2. A reel for the iron-wire, to be used for binding the necks of bottles and other vessels.
3. Shears and pincers for tying on the corks.
4. Machine for twisting iron-wire after it has been divided and cut to a proper length.

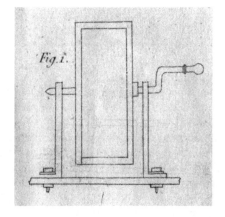

Reel for
iron-wire
(item 2
above)[139]

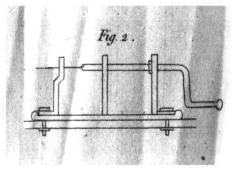

Machine for
twisting
iron-wire
(item 4 above)

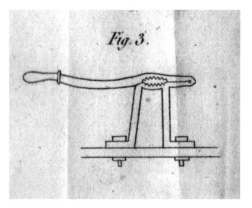

Instrument to
compress
corks
(item 5 above)

5. Two instruments forming a lever, and used for compressing and as it were biting the corks.
6. A bottle-boot or block, standing on three legs, and provided with a strong bat for corking.
7. A stool standing on five legs, for tying on the corks.
8. A sufficient quantity of linen bags, for covering the bottles and other vessels.
9. Two stools covered with leather and stuffed with hay, in order to shake the bottles upon them and in that way force a greater number of peas and other small substances into the bottles.
10. A press for the juice of plants, fruits and herbs; with pans, vessels, sieves, and everything else that belongs to it.

Nicolas's process started with thorough preparation of the food to be preserved, which included partially cooking it. The food was then carefully sealed inside a bottle or jar by means of a cork that had been well batted down, wired in place and then sealed with a paste. Each bottle was then put inside a linen bag and immersed to its neck in cold water inside a boiler. Nicolas used linen bags both to protect the bottles and to enable the mess created by any broken bottles to be cleared up more easily.

The water was then heated until it was boiling. The amount of time the food was to be in the boiling water varied. For example, green peas needed an hour and a half (or even two hours in a dry and hot season) while cauliflower required just 30 minutes. At the end of the given time, the heat was turned off and the water in the boiler was left to cool. 15 minutes later the water was drained off. It took a further two hours for the bottles to have sufficiently cooled for it to be safe to remove them from the boiler and stack them on racks.

At first, Nicolas obtained his supply of glass bottles from either *La Garre* or *Sèves* glass factories, both owned by his colleague from Ivry, M. Saget. However, by 1806 Nicolas had changed to glassware from *des Prémontrés*, a factory in Courcy-le-Château, a hundred miles away near Reims.[140]

By the time he was in Massy, Nicolas had been experimenting with his preserving techniques for over ten years and he was able to provide large quantities for sale. He already had some outlets, although not many records remain. On *20 frimaire an XII* (12 December 1803) Nicolas sold 60 bottles of vegetables to M. Benoist (possibly a relative of his wife's) in St. Petersburg, Russia. He charged M. Benoist a total of 212 *francs*. Two years later in December 1805 he sold 55 bottles of vegetables and broth for 170.60 *francs* to M. the Baron de Gohren, Grand Marshall of the Court of Bavaria.[141]

In 1803 Nicolas started to try to generate interest in his methods and so be able to sell to a wider market. In August 1803 he sent some bottled goods to the Maritime Prefect at Brest, asking that they be sent on board ship for a while before being tested for their freshness. Due to the British naval blockade, the ships could not actually do more than ride the waves in "the roads" outside the port. Nevertheless, the bottles remained on board for three months. At the end of that time, the five member Bureau of Health wrote the following report for General Caffarelli, the Maritime Prefect at Brest:

> The foods prepared according to the process of Citizen Appert and sent to this port by the Minister of the Navy, after a sojourn of three months lying in the roads, presented the following condition:
>
> The broth in bottles was good, the broth with boiled beef in a special vessel, good also, but weak; the boiled beef itself very edible.
>
> The beans and small peas, prepared both with and without meat, have all the freshness and the agreeable flavour of freshly picked vegetables.

Signed: Dubreuil
           Billard
           Duret
           Pichon
           Thaumer.
           & J. Miriel, the Secretary of the Council[142]

As a result, Nicolas was full of hope that orders would follow from the navy to provide nourishing provisions for the sick on board French ships. He explained in his 1810 book:

In the year 12 [1803 – 1804] having reason to hope that I should be employed to provide some nourishing provisions for the sick on board His Majesty's vessels, in consequence of some experiments which had already been made in the sea ports, by order of his Excellency the Minister of the Marine and Colonies, on food products preserved according to my method; I made the necessary arrangement for fulfilling the orders I had reason to expect. In consequence that I might not want too many bottles and jars, and that I might be able to condense the substance of eight messes in a bottle the size of one litre, I made the following experiment...[143]

Inexplicably, no order came.

By 1805 Nicolas had moved his shop from *N° 402 rue Neuve-Saint-Merry* to *N° 135 rue de la Verrerie*. The *rue de la Verrerie* is the name given to the *rue des Lombards* after its junction with the *rue St. Martin* and so Nicolas was very close to his original shop.

In 1805, Nicolas's produce was reviewed and praised for the first time in print. The 3rd edition of *L'Almanach des Gourmands*, by the impressively named Alexandre-Balthazar-Laurent Grimod de la Reynière, listed Nicolas's *dépôt* in the *rue de la Verrerie* with a short introductory paragraph:

It is at *rue de la Verrerie N° 135*, at the *Coquilles* corner, where the general store can be found with M. Appert's excellent bottled fruits and vegetables, which are the subject of a special article in this volume.[144]

Alexandre-Balthazar-Laurent Grimod de La Reynière[145]
(1758 – 1837)
Unknown artist.

Alexandre-Balthazar-Laurent Grimod de La Reynière is in many ways a strange figure for his time, but would not be out of place today. He was the first person to think and write about what makes good food, and where to go to sample the finest fare on offer. Originally he was a theatre critic, publishing his own work in the late 18th century. When he inherited a large fortune from his estranged father, he began to combine his love of good eating with his experience as a journalist. He published eight editions of his (approximately) annual *L'Almanach des Gourmands* from 1803 to 1812.

Nicolas does not feature in the first two editions (of 1803 and 1804), but does in each of the others.

Grimod de La Reynière's "special article" in his *Almanach* described both the factory at Massy and the fruits and vegetables on sale at Nicolas's shop:

> It was reserved for M. Appert, who has long engaged in this branch of commerce, to enable us to enjoy the many advantages of his method. He therefore bought a very large area of land in Massy, near Antony, four leagues from Paris. The land is excellent for vegetables, especially peas, beans, broad beans, etc... Here he has established his factory and all its operations. Employees pick the vegetables, bottling in all their freshness and goodness.
>
> There is no question of describing the process that preserves the food. We are only talking about the result, which is to have, at little cost, a wonderful sweet dish which reminds one of the month of May in the heart of winter, fooling even the most experienced cook. It is not an exaggeration to say that the peas especially are as green, tender and tasty as if they were being eaten in mid-season.[146]

The article goes on to list the produce that was available at *Nº 135 rue de la Verrerie*. As well as the peas, beans and broad beans mentioned above, he lists green beans, white beans, vegetable stock, currants, cherries, raspberries, plums, greengages, nectarines and peaches. But Nicolas's goods had a very special quality:

> The vegetables and fruits have the inestimable advantage of being able to be kept in their fresh state for a very long time. We saw some that had been kept fresh for several years...
>
> It is especially for long voyages and in northern countries where Nature does not provide such diversity... that M. Appert's preparations should be greatly sought. Before the war requests had come from the shores of the Baltic for that very purpose, although his goods are barely known in Paris. Now

that English tyranny has gripped the seas, declaring war on all commerce, these expeditions are extremely rare and difficult. Gourmands in Paris at least will then benefit by these inexpensive treats – bottled fruits and vegetables.[147]

Grimod de La Reynière's final recommendations from Nicolas's store are for "a very good Curaçao" and a liqueur which Nicolas had named "Extemporary," with which one "can make an excellent punch." In order to ensure that one bought the genuine Appert goods, Grimod instructed his readers to ensure that they checked for M. Appert's signature on the label.

Appert's signature,
guaranteeing genuine Appert contents[148]

In the following year's edition (1806) of *L'Almanach des Gourmands*, Grimod de La Reynière repeated much of his praise for Nicolas's preserved foods, describing Nicolas as bringing "spring and summer into the midst of the severest winter." He added that the Appert premises had moved from *rue de la Verrerie* to *rue du Four-Saint-Honoré, N° 12*.[149] This road is now known as the *rue Vauvilliers*, just off the main *rue Saint-Honoré* and not far from the Louvre.

Grimod encouraged people to go to the *rue du Four-*

Saint-Honoré, Nᵒ 12 "where he has opened a lovely shop, easy to distinguish by the ingenious picture he uses as a sign, and that we will merely indicate in order to stimulate rather than satisfy our readers' curiosity." Sadly, I cannot discover what the "ingenious picture he uses as a sign" was!

In 1806 Nicolas discovered how to treat milk so that it could be preserved in bottles. Grimod de La Reynière wrote:

We must place at the head of New Discoveries of 1806 the preserved milk by M. Appert. This skilful artist to whom we owe the pleasure of eating green peas in February, redcurrants in March, etc, not content with having changed the order of the seasons to benefit these delicacies, wanted to provide for sailors, for residents of southern countries and for all those that by their position are removed from cattle, a way to have at any time the milk of these animals, better than that sold in Paris, even smoother, creamier and sweeter than fresh milk.

After a multitude of tests, experiments and meditations that honour his chemical knowledge, M. Appert has finally succeeded. He sent to our Jury a bottle of milk that had been prepared more than six months before. We subjected it to various trials, which showed that the milk may be used... for the same domestic purposes as fresh milk. Although it has a slight yellow tint it is excellent, requiring less sugar than regular milk. Finally, it is far superior in all respects to Paris Milk, being almost of the consistency of what is currently sold under the name double cream.

Consider the delight of passengers, embarking on a long voyage, accustomed to having coffee with milk every morning so that it has become a real need due to habit, discovering this delight in the middle of the oceans! The inhabitants of hot countries who have been reduced to drinking goat's milk will rediscover cow's milk! Finally, in large towns and cities where it is almost impossible to obtain milk after a certain hour, the inhabitants would give all the world to be able to have some... This discovery is really valuable and deserves to be encouraged. [150]

In the autumn of 1805, during the time Nicolas was working on his method to preserve milk, France had started to slide into great financial difficulties. The particular catalyst was the collapse of the *Banque Récamier*, a renowned and very trusted institution. Withdrawals were suspended and panic started to set in. Jacques Récamier wrote to Napoleon, who was in the field in the days leading up to his greatest victory on 2 December 1805 at Austerlitz, just west of what is now Slavkov u Brna in the Czech Republic. Récamier requested a relatively small sum to bail the bank out and keep Paris and France solvent, but, flushed with his victory, Napoleon wrote back: "Is it at a time like this that I must be obliged to make advances to men who got themselves involved in bad business?"

Bankruptcies followed, taking in whole industries. Cash was in short supply and everywhere there were credit difficulties. To the list of bankruptcies, the name of Appert was added. On Tuesday 4 February 1806, Nicolas and Elisabeth Appert filed their names with the Civil Court of the Department of the Seine as bankrupts.[151] Their liabilities were an astonishing 138,493.80 *francs*! The list of creditors reads as a list of family and friends from Nicolas's past, testimony to the faith those who knew him well had in him. The list included:

Louis-Gervais, his brother, a caterer at Rethel;
Charles-Louis Limodin, his former associate in the Lombard Section;
Jean André Saget, the glass merchant from Ivry;
Messin, confectioner in Reims;
Jean-Baptiste Thuillier, a clerk at the Appert factory.

Against his liabilities, Nicolas had several assets: the factory, house and extensive farmland at Massy; his shop in Paris at *N° 12 rue du Four-Saint-Honoré*; and then of course there was all his stock, scattered around many retail outlets throughout the country.

Although Nicolas and Elisabeth did succeed in coming through the bankruptcy procedure it was doubtless accompanied by a loss of prestige and a reduction in goodwill among creditors. Nicolas also sold off several parts of his stock of equipment, including four large copper boilers, a tin-plated copper tub, three carts, a ladder and various minor items.[152] In the following year, Nicolas rented out part of the property at Massy to Jean-Baptiste Duchesne for 1,200 *francs* per year over six years.[153] This may be the same man who was in charge of Nicolas's Paris store, who was also named M. Duchesne.

By the summer of 1806, Nicolas was aged 56 and Elisabeth was 48. They faced the problems of making the factory profitable and paying off their creditors. Surprisingly, within four years business would be booming and Nicolas's name would be on the cover of his best-selling book. In 1808, looking back to Nicolas's position in 1806, Grimod de la Reynière wrote, referring to the whole range of preserved foods in Appert's store:

> You would think that such a discovery in France would excite the greatest admiration, and would earn him encouragement and reward from the authorities! On the contrary he has met obstacles on all sides and it has taken all the strength of spirit and all the drive with which M. Appert is gifted in order to overcome them.[154]

It was indeed going to take all that drive and strength of spirit that Grimod recognised and celebrated for Nicolas to recover financially.

APPERT (1749-1841) - Inventeur du procédé
de fabrication des conserves alimentaires

Detail from a Commemorative First Day Cover Envelope
5 March 1955

(From the author's collection)

Chapter 7

Massy: A Second Discovery 1806 – 1808

From Thursday 25 September to Sunday 19 October 1806 Nicolas took part in the fourth *L'Exposition de l'Industrie Française*, a large national exhibition of French industry and commerce. The first such Exhibition had been in the year VI (1798). This first gathering, marking the new spirit of enterprise and endeavour engendered by the Revolution, met for three days and took place on *le Champ de Mars*, Paris. There were just 110 exhibitors, with only French businesses being allowed to take part. The "French only" rule was rigorously adhered to for the next fifty years or so.

The popularity of *L'Exposition de l'Industrie Française* grew quickly, as it matched the spirit of the age where the French were fiercely proud of their nation and were constantly striving to be the best in Europe – especially in science, mathematics, technology and industry – and explicitly to be better than the English. The second Exhibition, in year IX (September 1801) took place in the courtyard of the Louvre and lasted for six days, attracting 220 exhibitors: doubling both indicators of success! The third Exhibition in year X (September 1802), just one year later, saw 540 *exposants* (exhibitors) over seven days.

By 1806 the Exhibition had returned to the *place des Invalides, Champ de Mars* in Paris. The event lasted for 24 days with an impressive 1422 exhibitors. Napoleon himself had attended the previous two Exhibitions and spoken with every exhibitor, but he did not attend in 1806 as he was busy in the field: the Battle of Jena where Napoleon defeated the Prussians under Frederick William III took place during the Exhibition on 14 October 1806.

There were 35 categories of exhibits, vying for the top award of a Gold Medal in each category. Nicolas, in the Food section, exhibited 32 bottles containing a variety of his produce (fruit, broth, vegetables and meat) all preserved by his own method.[155] Sadly, his contribution did not elicit any reaction at all from the 21 member jury, headed by the mathematician Gaspard Monge and including the famous scientist Joseph Louis Gay-Lussac.

The jury of illustrious French men in 1806 may not have credited the importance of Nicolas's discovery; however, he started to become news in journals, newspapers and other places. In the 1806 Exhibition, much attention had focused on the *département* from which the exhibitions had come. The French government believed that rivalry between regions could only increase the flow of innovation and improve France's ability to wage war. The Yearbook of Seine and Oise, the department in which Massy was situated, reviewed the contributions from their own region. In the 1807 edition of the Yearbook it said:

> There is a food shop for both the plant and animal kingdom at Massy, belonging to M. Appert, inventor of a new process to preserve for several years fruit and vegetables in their original state, and meat and broth in their freshness. He has a store in Paris at *N° 12 rue du Four-Saint-Honoré*. Samples of various products were exhibited at *La place des Invalides*.[156]

Over the winter of 1806 – 1807, Nicolas undertook a major journey to promote his preserved food. In an article entitled "Voyages of M. Appert," Grimod reported:

> [M. Appert] felt that even the very good consumption in Paris

of his various preparations was not enough to feed his huge factory, and that the North and the Navy could consume his products. The North being closed due to war, he had to rely entirely on the Navy, and try to get them to adopt for long voyages his fruit, vegetables, milk, broth and various meats – priceless objects at sea.

To achieve this, he took advantage of the winter season, during which his factory is idle, to visit our principal sea ports on the Ocean. Armed with letters of recommendation (for it is even necessary for the most skilful man to have these), he went successively to Nantes, Brest, Rochefort, La Rochelle, Bordeaux, etc, and there spoke with the competent authorities. He provided samples of all his preparations, encouraging the most rigorous examination, testing their merits or imperfections.[157]

After his journey, Nicolas followed up the contacts that he had made. He wrote to Rear-Admiral Allemand at *île-d'Aix* near La Rochelle and Rochefort, to whom he had sold some of his goods over a year before, no doubt asking for a testimonial regarding them. In March 1807 Nicolas received an official letter in reply. The Rear-Admiral wrote:

I communicated your letter, Sir, to the Captains, under my orders, and they tasted the day before yesterday the vegetables I purchased from you fourteen months ago, one bottle of which my *maitre-d'hôtel* had by accident left in the store room. As green peas and beans are just beginning to be gathered, the officers actually believed your preserved vegetables to be fresh, so well had you succeeded; they wish to purchase a large quantity of them, as well as soup, fruit, and meat in bottles. I shall also take a considerable quantity for myself at the end of the season.

I am so well persuaded, Sir, of the infinite advantage which would attend the provision of a quantity of articles for the use of the sick on board, that if his Excellency, the Minister of the Navy and Colonies, should do me the honour of asking for my opinion, I shall not hesitate to confirm this my opinion, as well for the sake of the government and of the sick, as of yourself. I shall take the earliest opportunity to speak with him on the subject. Accept assurance of my high consideration.

On board the Imperial ship *le Majestueux*,
at anchor off the *île-d'Aix*.

> Allemand
> 7 March 1807[158]

It is interesting that Rear-Admiral Allemand delayed two days after the food had been eaten before writing. No doubt he was waiting to be assured that the sailors suffered no ill effects.

During his journey, Nicolas had met Vice-Admiral Martin, the Maritime Prefect at Brest. The Vice-Admiral formed a committee to consider the merits of Appert's preserved food. The bottles were left on board a ship for five months before being examined by the committee. The report the committee produced was extremely positive:

It is demonstrated by everything just said that all the foods, loaded on board the *Stationnaire* on 12 December 1806 and brought ashore on 13 April 1807, and which were examined by a committee for that especial purpose, under the presidency of a commissary of the navy belonging to the hospitals, underwent no change while they were on board, and that they were found to be in the same state as they were initially at the first examination made at the beginning of the month of December last.

It may be added that M. Appert's process for the preservation of the articles examined has been followed by all the success he had himself promised; and that with improvement, which he considers to be very simple, and finding means to reduce the number of vessels employed, these provisions would offer great advantages on board His Majesty's and other vessels.[159]

Commemorative First Day Cover Postcard
5 March 1955

(From the author's own collection)

On Monday 27 April 1807 Nicolas replied to Vice-Admiral Martin. He must have been very pleased with this report from the committee and was no doubt hoping that the Vice-Admiral would be interested in actually placing orders with him. It seemed that everyone thought well of his products, but no-one took the next logical step: to provision the fleet with them. On 22 May 1807, Vice-Admiral Martin replied from Rochefort:

> I have received, Sir, your letter of the 27th of last April. According to your desire, I have addressed to his Excellency, the Minister of the Navy and Colonies, a report of the examination of a variety of provisions prepared according to your process.
>
> I shall neglect no opportunity of making known a discovery which appears to be as useful to the State as it is interesting to sailors. I have the honour to salute you.
>
> *Le vice-amiral, préfet marine*
> Martin[160]

At around the same time, a separate committee of investigation at Bordeaux, commissioned by the Prefect of the Department, also reported on its findings. A section of their report is quoted in Nicolas's book:

> The detail which we have just given, on the objects prepared by M. Appert, will point out to you that they were in a state of perfect preservation; that the means made use of do not depend on the addition of extraneous substances, and that these means are founded on a process invented or improved by M. Appert, which do not destroy the aroma or flavour of the subjects submitted to their influence.[161]

To give an idea of the size of Nicolas's business at this point, Grimod de La Reynière wrote that in 1807 the Appert factory at Massy produced and preserved twenty thousand bottles of peas.[162] In all, the Appert factory must have produced towards a quarter of a million bottles a year when the variety of their produce is considered: green peas, green beans, broad beans, white beans, cherries, apricots, peaches, plums, broth, milk, clarified whey; every kind of meat and game, poultry and various types of fish.

Grimod de La Reynière continued to promote Nicolas's work in each of his publications. In the 1808 sixth edition of his *Almanach* he wrote:

> Praises are due to the admirable methods of this ingenious manufacturer, by whose art is reproduced under the ice of winter all the treasures of the summer, autumn and spring... It is a type of food industry that honours France and that deserves to be better promoted. He also stocks bottled Champagne and Bordeaux, and "Extemporary." M. Duchesne is at the head of the store.[163]

At Massy, Nicolas had almost half an acre of vines. Around September/October 1808, when the grape harvest was at its height, Nicolas's thoughts might have turned back to his time in Bordeaux in the previous winter. The marvellous local wines could not find a wider market because they did not travel at all well. In fact, often the wines turned to vinegar in the cellars where they were made.

Nicolas wondered whether his heating methods could be adapted to solve this problem. He experimented with the temperature of the water used and the length of time the wine was to be heated. As with the preservation of food in bottles, Nicolas proceeded with determination and method.

This, Nicolas's second major discovery, is best described in his own words from the 1831 fourth edition of his book. The method he devised would be rediscovered just over 50 years later by another Frenchman, Louis Pasteur, and would henceforward be known as pasteurization. The processes were not finalised by Nicolas until after his 1810 book went to print and so were not included in that first edition. Nicolas, looking back in 1831, wrote:

In 1808, in the time of the grape-harvests, I took the black grapes, picked from the vine with care; after having removed the rotten grapes and those that were green, I peeled them, next I put them through a sieve; I then put them under the press that was located next to the sieves, in order to extract what juice remained; I combined the sieve with a barrel. After leaving it resting thus twenty-four hours, I put it in bottles, etc., to give it a good boiling in the boiler. When my operation was finished, I withdrew the bottles from the boiler. I stored them in my laboratory, on the laths, as one normally places wine.

At the harvest of 1810, I repeated the same experiment on about eight hundred pints of grape must prepared with the same care and attention.

A quarter was bottled without any preparation. Another quarter was purified and bottled. The third quarter was purified, de-acidified, and bottled. The fourth quarter was purified, de-acidified, heated to twenty degrees of the hydrometer, and bottled. All were well sealed, etc, and put into the boiler for boiling.

I then laid them on the laths in my cellar.

No-one is unaware that of the wines of France, the most delicate, notably those of Burgundy, cannot bear even the shortest sea trip. The susceptibility of a few of these wines is so great that we are often obliged to consume them in the country where they are harvested by the impossibility of risking transport without spoiling them completely.

At the time when the introduction of French wines was prohibited by land in the kingdom of the Netherlands, the owners of these vineyards were plunged into despair. The House of Beaune, with whom I maintained relations, asked me to look for ways to preserve wines of this vintage during long journeys. Before long they sent me a basket of bottles to be devoted to my experiments. Motivated by a noble desire to be useful to my country and always full of confidence in the effect of heat, I set to work and did not delay in finding a solution to the problem.

Here is how I obtained it: the bottles that were sent to me were badly corked and too full. I withdrew a little wine in order to leave a gap of 3 cm in the neck; I re-corked hermetically and tied two wires across it. Afterwards I put it in the water-bath and raised the heat only to 70 degrees, fearing to alter the colour.

Fifteen days later, I sent to one of my contacts in Le Havre twelve bottles of this wine with the request that several captains of ships be entrusted with one for a long journey and then to retrieve them for me so that they could be tasted. In order to compare them on their return I retained a certain number of the bottles which had undergone the same operation as those I was sending on board, and for a second comparison I put some aside just as I had received them from Beaune.

I waited more than two years for the return of my bottles; of six that my contact dispatched on a long voyage, only two returned from St. Domingo. Very curious, as you can well imagine, to know the result of such an important experiment I hurried to submit one of these bottles to tasting by a skilful connoisseur. He compared it with two others, namely one that had remained in my correspondent's cellar in Le Havre and that he had recently sent back to me, and another of the ones that I had preserved intact. The result of this triple comparison was extraordinary and showed that this wine, originally the same, presented three essentially different qualities.

The bottle kept at my home and that had not undergone the preparation, had a very unripe taste; the bottle sent back from Le Havre had retained its flavour; but the superiority of the one returned from St. Domingo was infinite, nothing equalled its sophistication and bouquet, the delicacy of its taste much superior to that from Le Havre, and far better than mine. One year later I had the satisfaction of repeating this experiment with equal success.

It is therefore undoubtedly shown by these facts, as clearly as it could be, that one can, with a very simple preparation, export our fine wines to the farthest reaches of the globe; but even if my process did not have this invaluable advantage, as it does, what value has it for France itself, where there are so many cellars in which our best wines cannot be preserved even in bottles? Let us hope therefore that this simple procedure that I have just succinctly described will soon be generally adopted, and that its infallibility together with its inexpensiveness will encourage many owners to make the attempt.[164]

Unfortunately, the method did not become generally known and its use lapsed. Pasteur came to the same conclusions, describing his methods in his 1866 book *Études sur le vin*. He wrote of Appert:

When I first published the results of my experiments on the possible preservation of wine by prior heating, it was evident that I was only making a new application of Appert's method, but I was completely unaware that Appert had long before thought of the same application... It is nevertheless this skilful industrialist and manufacturer who, at first, clearly indicated the possibility of preserving wine by applying heat ...

For me, the merit that I claim is to have found the very real virtue of Appert's method applied to wines, by rigorous experimental demonstrations and using the principles of scientific deduction.[165]

In January 1809, Nicolas made arguably the most important decision of his life as an inventor. He went to *la rue du Bac*, at that time the home of *La Société d'Encouragement pour l'Industrie Nationale*, in order to see if he could interest them in his work.

Commemorative postcard issued 18 September 2010

Artwork by Roland Irolla (1935 –)

Below: Text from the reverse

(From the author's collection)

2010 Année Nicolas Appert déclarée célébration nationale.
Bicentenaire de la publication de sa découverte : l'appertisation.
Nicolas Appert né à Châlons-en-Champagne
le 17 novembre 1749.
Fils d'aubergiste, en 1795 il invente la conservation des aliments
en les chauffant au bain-marie dans des bouteilles
hermétiquement fermées.
Il meurt à Massy le 1er juin 1841.

L'ART DE CONSERVER,

PENDANT PLUSIEURS ANNÉES,

TOUTES LES SUBSTANCES ANIMALES ET VÉGÉTALES;

Ouvrage soumis au Bureau consultatif des Arts et
Manufactures, revêtu de son approbation, et publié
sur l'invitation de S. Exc. le Ministre de l'Intérieur.

Par APPERT,

*Propriétaire à Massy, département de Seine et Oise,
ancien Confiseur et Distillateur, Élève de la bouche de
la Maison ducale de Christian IV.*

« J'ai pensé que votre découverte méritait
» un témoignage particulier de la bienveillance
» du Gouvernement. »
Lettre de S. Exc. le Ministre de l'Intérieur.

A PARIS,

Chez PATRIS et Cie, Imprimeurs-Libraires, quai
Napoléon, au coin de la rue de la Colombe, n° 4.

1810.

Title page from Nicolas's book

Chapter 8

Into Print: "*L'art de conserver...*" 1809 – 1810

*L*a Société d'Encouragement pour l'Industrie Nationale had been created by the Three Consuls on *9 brumaire an* X (31 October 1801) under the presidency of Jean-Antoine Chaptal, with a view to developing all aspects of industrial and economic life in France. It is still going strong today, and its most recent *plaquette* (booklet) mentions Appert twice![166]

In January 1809, Nicolas took several of his preserved goods to the Society, most of them dating back to August 1808, the end of the previous season. In response, the Society set up a "Special Commission, on vegetable and animal substances, preserved by M. Appert." The committee of three – Denis-Placide Bouriat, Antoine Augustin Parmentier and Louis-Bertrand Guyton-Morveau – set to work on their analysis and report. Nicolas had to wait until after the March meeting of the Society before hearing their conclusions.

Meanwhile, Nicolas obtained more positive publicity. In *Le Courrier de l'Europe* of Friday 10 February 1809 it was reported that "M. Appert has found the art of fixing the seasons. In his store spring, summer and autumn live in bottles like those delicate plants that a gardener protects with a glass dome against the seasonal weather."[167]

Then on 28 February 1809 the *Journal du Commerce* reported that Nicolas's preserves improved the health of sailors.[168] Was Nicolas at last on the point of a breakthrough with the authorities?

Two weeks later, on Wednesday 15 March 1809, M. Bouriat read the Special Commission's report to the Council of Administration of the Society. The text was later published in the Society's *Bulletin de la Société d'Encouragement pour l'Industrie Nationale, N° 58* (April 1809)[169] and a briefer version was included in the *Archives des Découvertes et des Inventions Nouvelles Pendant L'Année 1809.*[170]

The report is also given in the preface of the 1810 edition of Nicolas's book. Below I have given the 1812 translation from the English edition, printed in London by Black, Parry and Kingsbury:[171]

> The council referred to a committee, consisting of Messrs. Guyton-Morveau, Parmentier and myself [M. Bouriat], the examination of vegetable and animal substances presented by M. Appert, and preserved by his process, for more than eight months.
>
> These substances were:
>
> 1. *Pot-au-feu* [a French dish of boiled meat, fowls, etc]
> 2. *Consommé*
> 3. Milk
> 4. Whey
> 5. Green peas
> 6. Small Windsor Beans
> 7. Cherries
> 8. Apricots
> 9. Currant Juice
> 10. Raspberries
>
> Each of these articles was contained in an earthen vessel hermetically sealed, the cork being fastened with iron wire and sealed with pitch. Proceeding methodically with our enquiry:
>
> We found in the *pot-au-feu* a jelly tolerably rich, with a piece of beef and two pieces of fowl in the middle. Warming

the whole with care, to a suitable degree, the soup was found good, and the meat which was separated from it, very tender, and of an agreeable flavour.

The *consommé* appeared to us to be excellent; and though prepared fifteen months before; there was scarcely any discernible difference between its then state, and what it would have been, if made fresh on the same day.

The milk was found to be of a yellowish colour, resembling that of colostrum or beestings, more savoury than ordinary milk: a superiority it derives from the concentration it has undergone. It may be affirmed that milk of this kind, though prepared nine months before, may supply the place of the greater part of the cream sold at Paris. What however will appear more extraordinary is, that this same milk having been put into a pint bottle which was uncorked a month before, to take out part of it, and re-corked afterwards with little care, was also preserved, having undergone scarcely any change. At first it appeared to have somewhat thickened, but a slight shaking was sufficient to bring back its ordinary liquidity. I present it here in the same bottle, that you may convince yourselves of a fact, which I should have had difficulty to believe, if I had heard of it only, without having the evidence before me.

The whey which we afterwards examined, presented some singular appearances not less astonishing. It had all the transparency of whey recently prepared. Its colour was deeper, it had a stronger taste, and it was somewhat thicker. It underwent a change also with less rapidity, having been exposed to the air at the end of a fortnight; for a bottle opened six weeks ago, occasionally shaken, and ill corked, did not begin to lose its transparency till the end of a fortnight. Its surface at the end of more than a month was covered with a somewhat thick mouldiness, which was then carefully taken off, left the remainder still possessing the flavour of whey.

The green peas and the Windsor beans, boiled with the attention enjoined by M. Appert, furnished two excellent dishes, which the remoteness of the usual season of such vegetables appeared to render still more finely flavoured and agreeable.

Whole cherries and apricots cut in quarters preserved a great part of the flavour they had when gathered. It is true M. Appert was obliged to gather them before they were quite ripe, lest they should lose too much of their figure in the glass jars in which they were preserved.

The currant and raspberry juice appeared to us to enjoy almost all their qualities. We found the aroma of the raspberry perfectly preserved, as well as the somewhat aromatic acid of the currant. Their colour was only a little faded.

Whether about taste, colour or aroma, the committee had only praise to heap upon the preserved foods that they tested. M. Bouriat summed up the first part of the report with:

Such were the results of our examining the substances prepared according to M. Appert's process, more than eight months, and some of them a year, and fifteen months before; for instance the whey. We could only receive his statement as to the time of the previous preparation of these articles, as they had been deposited but two months with the Society; but even this shorter period is sufficient to give us a favourable opinion of the author's process... M. Appert forwarded to the Council mere specimens of the articles I have enumerated; but he prepares a still greater variety of alimentary substances. He did not communicate his process to us.

The report compared the results of Nicolas's process with the various ways that people had attempted to prolong the usefulness of stored food previously:

Desiccation, ardent spirits, acids and oils, saccharine and saline substances, &c, have been made use of; but it must be confessed that these means cause many productions to lose a part of their properties, or otherwise modifies them, so that their aroma and flavour are no longer to be recognized. From this point of view the process of M. Appert appears to us preferable, if without desiccation he adds no extraneous substance to that he wishes to preserve. There is every reason to believe that his method is by so much the better, as the substances on which he operates are more capable of sustaining so high a temperature without a sensible change...

The report concluded:

It is apparent...that the process of M. Appert is as certain as it is useful. It affords the means of enjoying throughout the empire, during the whole year, and with great convenience, the productions which belong alone to a part of it, without fearing that they may have undergone any change by their having been transported to a great distance, or from the remoteness of the season of their growth. Merely under this point of view, the advantage appears to be great ...

The process of this manufacturer is not less valuable in the sparing of sugar in the use of fruit... It may be further adddded that the flavour and aroma of substances are better preserved by M. Appert's process, than by the decoctions usually made use of in order to preserve them with sugar. This will be considered a very great advantage, when we reflect how prodigious a quantity of this colonial produce is every year employed to preserve the different kinds of fruit and their juices. The establishment of M. Appert has not perhaps been duly appreciated by rich capitalists, who might have given it that desirable extension which it will only gradually receive, if the author is abandoned to his own resources...

The experiments already made on board several vessels, prove that the sick among the crew will be well satisfied with M. Appert's preparations, which furnish them with the means of procuring, when necessary, meat and broth of a good quality, milk, acid fruits, and even anti-scorbutic juices; for M. Appert assures us that he is able to preserve these also.

With respect to the embarkation of meat necessary for a whole crew on a long voyage, a slight difficulty seems to lie in the requisite multiplicity of bottles. But M. Appert will, without doubt, find means to obviate this inconvenience, by the choice of containers less fragile and of a larger size.

Our opinion of the substances preserved by M. Appert, and transmitted to our examination, is, that they were all of good quality; that they may be made use of without any inconvenience; and that the Society owes great praise to the author for having so far advanced the art of preserving vegetable and animal substances. We are happy to render this homage to the zeal and disinterestedness with which he has laboured to attain his end...

The Council concurred with the committee's findings. The *Société d'Encouragement pour l'Industrie Nationale's* Secretary, Mathieu de Montmorency, subsequently wrote to Nicolas:

Paris
7 April 1809
Sir,

I have the pleasure to transmit to you a copy of the Report made to the *Société d'Encouragement,* by Messrs. Guyton-Morveau, Parmentier and Bouriat, on your preserved vegetable and animal substances. Nothing can be added to the judgment passed by the Committee on your discovery. They announce, that it has not been in their power to make any experiments either sufficiently exact, or continued for a sufficient length of time, to enable them to verify to what extent the substances prepared by you may be preserved; but what they have themselves observed, suffices to enable them to form an opinion to which they were previously disposed, by the numerous and decisive testimonies which attest your success.

The Society is of the opinion that they are rendering a service to the country and humanity, when they make known so useful a discovery with the eulogies which it merits. Their desire will be accomplished, should their suffrage determine the public to make use of your productions, and so contribute to confer upon you the just rewards of your labours.

Accept, Sir, the assurance of the perfect respect with which I have the honour to salute you.

Math. Montmorency
Secretary, &c.[172]

In his correspondence with the Society for the Encouragement of National Industry, Nicolas had not given any details of the actual process of preserving food. At this stage, Nicolas must have been hoping for enough publicity due to the high profile backing of the Society to make a difference to his level of sales. He had 10 retail outlets apart from his shop in Paris, all in the region he had visited two years earlier. They were listed in the Society's bulletin accompanying the committee's report. They were:

Bordeaux :	Mm. Dierx and Paton, *rue des Argentiers* and M. Quinton, *place de la Bourse*
Brest:	M. Pity, *N° 46 rue de la Rampe*
La Rochelle:	M. Chatelain, opposite *La Poissonnerie*
L'Orient :	M. Macé, *place de la Réunion*
Morlaix :	Mm. Punchera & Co, *rue des Arts*
Nantes :	M. Lizé, *N° 24 rue de la Fosse*
Quimper :	M. Jacques Pity, *rue Saint-François*
Rennes :	M. Vignon, *rue de l'Horloge*
Vannes :	M. Maurice, *rue Porte-Prison*

On Wednesday 10 May 1809, Nicolas's oldest – and favourite – brother Louis-Gervais died. He was aged 69 and had been a *traiteur* (caterer) at Rethel, about 40 miles north of Châlons.[173] This left just three of Nicolas's close family still alive: Nicolas himself aged 59, Jules-Claude-Marie aged 62, and the youngest brother Jean-Baptiste aged 56.

Nicolas and Elisabeth's oldest child had reached his 23rd birthday. Charles-Pierre-Nicolas may have worked in the family business at Massy for a while, but he became a *professeur* (teacher). Possibly he was away from home studying at this time. Elisabeth-Marie-Nicole was aged 22; Aglaë-Françoise was 20; my wife's great-great-great-grandmother Amélie-Justine was almost 16; and Angélique-Eloïse was 14. It would be fascinating to know what their daily life entailed, but no record has been left.

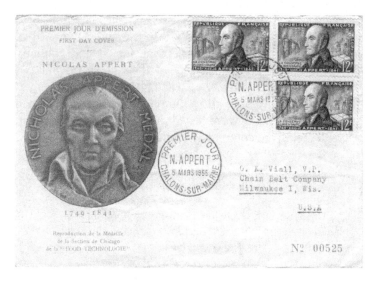

Commemorative First Day Cover Envelope
showing the bronze Nicholas (sic) Appert Medal
awarded annually from 1942 by the
Chicago Section of the Institute of Food Technologists

5 March 1955

(From the author's collection)

On Monday 15 May 1809, Nicolas wrote to the Minister of the Interior, Jean-Pierre Bachesson, the *Comte de Montalivet*. No doubt emboldened by the report from the Society for the Encouragement of National Industry, Nicolas asked for aid in further developing his discovery.[174] Montalivet asked the *Bureau Consultatif des Arts et Manufactures* (Advisory Board of Arts and Manufacturing) to investigate Nicolas's preserves.

Before this committee had concluded its work, the Agricultural Society met on Wednesday 21 June 1809 and, in Nicolas's words, "made an appeal to the whole nation, in order to collect all the information and documents which might contribute to the composition of a work on the art of preserving, by the best possible means, every kind of food." In the 1831 4th edition of his book, Nicolas gives an extract from the records of this meeting of the Agricultural Society of the Department of the Seine:[175]

The art of preserving food substances is still far from having received the degree of perfection and development to which it is susceptible, and it is desirable to achieve this progress because of the great advantages that would result for various classes of society.

It happens that several commodities, such as fruits, vegetables, fish, meat, etc, which are very abundant in certain seasons or in certain districts, are wasted and sold cheaply, while in other circumstances, they might double and quadruple in value, and even be impossible to obtain, because we have not used the means of preservation by which it would have been possible to prolong their duration. Using these means, several of these commodities for which there is no market and which are consumed at almost no profit, would enter into the general mass of subsistence, and supply the table of the poor and the rich throughout the year, with an abundance and variety of dishes which would increase significantly the livelihood of the first and multiply the enjoyment of the second.

Those who have applied themselves to the particular needs of this part of the domestic economy are aware of the resources it then gives them in their household, and they know how much the public would benefit if it was generally put into practice;

but what has been published on this subject is too incomplete and too inaccurate to serve as a guide.

Based on these considerations, the Agricultural Society of the Department of the Seine thought that the publication of a special book on *The Art of Preserving Food Substances* could only be extremely useful, both for society and for individuals. Consequently the Society has invited one of its members, M. de Lasteyrie, who had already been occupied with this subject, to continue the research and experiments already begun, and in order to enable him to complete his work, the Society has resolved to invite all its members and its contacts, both foreign and domestic, to be in correspondence with its secretary, under the auspices of His Excellency the Minister of the Interior, or to communicate directly to M. de Lasteyrie himself any processes of preservation that they may know of.

The Society hereby indicates the general nature of the information it wants:

1st The Company asks for a description of commonly used methods in your locality for the preservation of grain, flour, vegetables, roots, herbs, fruit, fish, milk, butter, cheese, eggs, meat (birds or animals), and so on.

2nd As we can rely only on a process that has been shown by experiments repeated several times, people who wish to send information are asked to describe only preservation methods whose effectiveness has been recognized by their own experience or that of other people worthy of trust.

3rd If the processes used in a locality have been described in some book, simply indicate the page of the book where this is described. Further, note any improvements to these processes.

4th Several good preservation methods have been published in German, English, Dutch, Swedish and Danish books. The Society invites those who know of these to give an indication of them if they are assured of the benefits of these methods.

5th The information requested covers all kinds of processes, performed on either large or small amounts, for the preservation of various food substances for humans and even that of animals. These are usually salting, drying, smoking, milling, etc, the use of vinegar, oil, butter, fat, honey, sugar, etc, deprivation of contact with air, light, etc.

6th Do not forget to describe the qualities of various substances used in food preservation, the nature and size of vessels and utensils, the position and construction of apparatus for this particular preservation and the operations that precede it.

Signed,
Le sénateur comte François De Neufchâteau (*président*)
& M. Silvestre (*secrétaire*).

The Agricultural Society made this request public on Saturday 15 July 1809 by writing to all their members and correspondents. Nicolas received a copy of the letter from the Secretary of the Agricultural Society of the Department of the Seine:[176]

Sir,
I have the honour to send you herewith a decree of the Agricultural Society of the Department of the Seine, relating to information that it seeks regarding the compilation of a book on the art of preserving food substances. This work is at one and the same time needed by commerce, navy and domestic economy. The Society hopes that you will be able to assist in its implementation, by communicating to it the various processes that you may know of.
I have the honour to greet you with marked esteem,

Silvestre.

Nicolas wrote of his reaction to this letter in his 1810 book:[177]

It was after invitations of so great weight that I resolved to make known a method of effecting this object, of great facility in the execution, and at the same time very cheap, and which, by the extension it admits of, may afford numerous advantages to society.

This was a momentous decision, and one that not only changed the course of Nicolas's life, but can be said without exaggeration to have changed that of history too.

What is particularly interesting is that most descriptions of Nicolas's achievements – in encyclopaedias and biographical dictionaries – say that he put his mind to the task after Napoleon's government offered a large reward for anyone who could solve the problem. Here is an example from Wikipedia:[178]

> In 1795 the French military offered a cash prize of 12,000 *francs* for new method to preserve food. After some 14 or 15 years of experiment, Appert submitted his invention and won the prize in January 1810.

However, the evidence from the time contained in Nicolas's book, written in 1810, does not mention any offer of a prize from Napoleon in 1795, or any other year. It seems, rather, that the request for information that would lead to a solution of the problem was the one made by the Agricultural Society of the Department of the Seine in 1809. Nicolas then decided to share his knowledge, already gained from twenty years of experimenting, and as a result the government decided to give him the "standard" reward for "the inventors of useful processes." Therefore the reward Nicolas received in due course – 12,000 *francs* – was indeed from the French government, but it was not as a specified prize that had been announced beforehand, but rather as a reward for and recognition of his achievement.

This interpretation of events is corroborated by a French government report, *"Rapports du Jury sur L'Exposition Universelle Internationale de 1889: Viande et poissons, légumes et fruits,"* which describes the sequence of events as I have portrayed them, and does not mention a prize as Nicolas's motivation to begin work on preserving foods.[179]

On Saturday 29 July 1809, the committee of *le Bureau Consultatif des Arts et Manufactures* that the Minister of the Interior, the *Comte de Montalivet*, had set up in May reported to the Board. The committee had been extremely impressed with Nicolas's preserves and it "thinks that the petitioner has some rights to benefits from the government and that as he seems willing to allow society the fruit of his discovery, he should be given 6,000 *francs* both as an incentive and as compensation."[180]

Two weeks later, on Friday 11 August 1809, the *Comte de Montalivet* wrote to Nicolas. He put forward two methods by which Nicolas could proceed: either to take out a *brevet d'invention* (a patent, which would bring Nicolas royalties from its use) or to publish his process for all to use freely. Nicolas wrote later of his decision:

> Finding the latter means nobler and more in keeping with my character, and especially more likely to serve humanity, I preferred that a commission be named and that I expounded to it every means of preparation.[181]

Subsequently, the matter was referred back to the *Bureau Consultatif des Arts et Manufactures* for a more comprehensive investigation. At the Board's meeting of Thursday 24 August 1809 a commission of four eminent scientists was set up, consisting of Philibert Bardel, Scipion-Perrier, Pierre-Claude Molard and Joseph Louis Gay-Lussac.

We have met M. Gay-Lussac before, as a member of the jury for the 1806 *L'Exposition de l'Industrie Française*. Since then, in 1808, Gay-Lussac and his fellow professor at the École Polytechnique in Paris, Louis Jacques Thénard, had isolated the element that came to be known as boron; a feat independently achieved by Sir Humphry Davy in England at much the same time.

The commission journeyed to Massy on Saturday 9

September 1809 to see first hand "the place of residence of M. Appert and in which are established his workshops." More importantly, Nicolas then prepared, as they watched, all the things that were to be preserved. Then Nicolas explained his process, showing them how he preserved chicken, mutton, veal broth, a variety of fish, mushrooms, peas, artichokes, broad beans, milk, whey, and more.

After each of the preparations, the commission fixed seals to the products on a total of 62 jars and bottles. These jars and bottles were then placed in baskets and locked under seal in a storeroom in Nicolas's factory in Massy for thirty days.[182]

The commission travelled back to Massy after the thirty days were up, on Thursday 12 October 1809. They checked the seals and when they were satisfied that all was in order, Nicolas uncorked each bottle. The scientists examined the contents carefully and thoroughly. Back in Paris, they wrote their report for His Excellency, the Count of Montalivet, Minister of the Interior:

> *Monseigneur,*
>
> We have carried out the examination following Your Excellency's instructions and with the closest attention, since the results we are publishing seem most extraordinary, even to ourselves. We are convinced of the simplicity and accuracy of the process, and we can maintain that M. Appert communicated with all of us without restraint and with the utmost frankness.
>
> He gave us a complete description of his procedures and is committed to providing any subsequent clarification that we need to ask of him. We believe that he is entitled to a reward from the government; we propose that Your Excellency grant him 12,000 *francs* as both compensation for the communication he has made to us and as an encouragement.[183]

The *Bureau Consultatif des Arts et Manufactures* met in full session on Thursday 4 January 1810 and heard and approved the full report. Following that meeting, Montalivet wrote to Nicolas with the good news that not only did the commission validate his process, but that the 12,000 *franc* grant was to be made – on one condition. Montalivet wrote:

My Board of Arts and Manufacturing has reported to me, Sir, the examination it has made of your process for the preservation of fruits, vegetables, meat, soup, milk, etc, and from that report no doubt can be entertained of the success of this process. As the preservation of animal and vegetable substances may be of the utmost utility in sea voyages, in hospitals and domestic economy, I deem your discovery worthy of an especial mark of the goodwill of the government. I have in consequence acceded to the recommendation made me by my council to grant you a recompense of 12,000 *francs*. In so doing I had in view assigning to you the reward due to the inventors of useful processes, and also indemnifying you for the expenses you have been obliged to incur, either in forming your establishment or in the experiments necessary to establish the success of your process. You shall be immediately informed when you may repair to the public treasury and receive the 12,000 *francs*.

It appears to me of importance, Sir, that you should spread the knowledge of your preserving process. I desire, therefore, that agreeably to your own proposal, you will digest a detailed and exact description of your process. This description, which you will remit to my Board of Arts and Manufacturing, shall be printed at your expense, after it shall have been examined. You will then transmit me 200 copies. The transmission of these copies being the only condition I impose on you for the payment of the 12,000 *francs*, I doubt not you will hasten to fulfil it. I desire, Sir, you will acknowledge receipt of my letter.

Accept assurances, &c,
Montalivet[184]

It took less than two months for Nicolas to write his book.

He submitted it, as requested, to the *Bureau Consultatif des Arts et Manufactures*, who approved it and wrote a letter certifying their approval to be included in Nicolas's book:

> The undersigned members of the Board of Arts and Manufacturing attached to the Minister of the Interior, being required by His Excellency to examine the description of the process of M. Appert for the preservation of food, certify that the details it contains, both the mode of carrying out the process and its results, are exactly conformable to the various experiments which M. Appert has made before them, by order of His Excellency.
>
> Signed by Bardel, Gay-Lussac, Scipion-Perrier & Molard.
> Paris
> 19 April 1810[185]

The book was published by Patris et Cie, printers and booksellers, at *Quai Napoléon, N° 4 rue de la Colombe, dans la Cité, Paris*. This first edition of *Le Livre de Tous Les Ménages, ou L'art de conserver pendant plusieurs années toutes les substances animales et végétales* ran to 6,000 copies. It had 148 pages and was produced in octavo, i.e. with a whole single sheet folded three times to form eight leaves. The book also contained a set of engravings by N. L. Rousseau showing the various tools and other pieces of equipment used in the process of preservation. The book sold for 3 *francs* or 3.50 *francs* by post. This was the first of four editions to be made during Nicolas's lifetime, not counting translations.

In order to obtain an idea of the breadth and depth of Nicolas's book, it is useful to consider the *Table Des Matières*, or contents list. Following various extracts of correspondence and the certificate of approval quoted above, the book starts on its main matter:

The art of conserving animal and vegetable substances
Description of laboratories and workshops
Of bottles and vessels
Of corks
Of corking
The means of distinguishing defective bottles
Description of the Author's process applied to:

    Boiled meat
    Gravy
    Broth, or jelly
    Round of beef, fillet of mutton, fowls and young partridges
    New-laid eggs
    Milk
    Cream
    Whey
    Vegetables
    Green Peas
    Asparagus
    Windsor beans
    Peeled Windsor beans
    French beans
    Artichokes
    Cauliflowers
    Sorrel
    Spinach, chicory and other herbs
    A soup called Julienne
    A vegetable soup
    Tomatoes
    Herbs and medicinal plants
    The juices of herbs
    Fruits and their juices
    White and red currants in bunches
    White and red currants stripped
    Cherries, raspberries and mulberries
    Juice of redcurrants
    Strawberries
    Apricots

Peaches and nectarines
Prunes from greengages and plums
Pears of every kind
Chestnuts, truffles and mushrooms
The juice of grapes or must

Of the mode of making use of the substances which have been preserved;

Meat, game, poultry and fish
Jellies made of meat and poultry
Milk and cream
Vegetables
French beans
Peas, beans, etc
Spinach and chicory
Vegetable soups
Tomatoes and herbs
Preserved fruits, marmalades, etc
Currant jam
Syrup of currants
Ices
Cordials
Chestnuts, truffles and mushrooms
Grape juice, or must
Preparation of grape syrup
Syrups and ratafias

General observations
Practical remarks
Letter from the Secretary of the Society for the Encouragement of National Industry
Report of the Society

As can readily be seen, Nicolas provided his readers with a comprehensive list regarding the correct preparation and use of a wide variety of foods. As an example of the instructions given, here is (in its entirety) one of the smaller sections, that on "white and red currants in bunches"

I gather the white and red currants apart and not too ripe. I collect the finest, and in the finest bunches; and I bottle them, taking care to shake them down on the stool, in order to fill up any gaps in the bottle. Then I cook them, etc, in order to put them in the water-bath which I am careful to watch closely; and as soon as I perceive it boils, I withdraw the fire rapidly, and a quarter of an hour afterwards draw off the water from the bath by means of the cock, etc.[186]

Nicolas's book began to make quite a stir. On 21 May 1810 the *Journal de Paris* told its readers: "thanks to the talent of a skilful chemist, everyone can prepare for themselves in season when nature is prodigal with her treasures, the fruits and vegetables that she refuses and we would love to enjoy in the off-season. Passengers may carry from one hemisphere to the other excellent broth and milk as fresh as if from the dairy. Sailors no longer need fear scurvy!"[187]

The next day the *Journal du commerce, de politique et de littérature* carried news of Nicolas's book.[188] A month later, on 22 June 1810, the *Journal de l'Empire* wrote that the *Bureau Consultatif des Arts et Manufactures* had awarded M. Appert "an encouragement" of 12,000 *francs* both as a reward for his invention and also to defray costs of his work. The book, it continued, contained "an exact and detailed description of all the processes of M. Appert."[189]

On the following day in Nicolas's home town, the "Journal of Announcements and News of Châlons-sur-Marne" told its readers of the book and its price. The following week it reprinted the article from the *Journal de l'Empire*.[190]

Most of the 200 copies that Nicolas sent to the *Bureau des Arts et Manufactures* were sent out, on 27 June 1810, by order of the Minister of the Interior, to each of the 130 or so prefects of the French Departments. The instructions from Paris were to make the discovery known as quickly as possible so that people could begin to benefit from it straight away.[191]

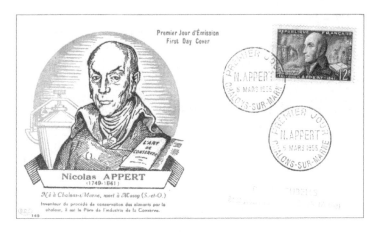

Commemorative First Day Cover Envelope
5 March 1955

(From the author's collection)

In *Le Bulletin de pharmacie* of Monday 2 July 1810 M. Parmentier, member of the *Institut de France*, the leading pharmacist of the Armies of France, and one of the members of the investigating committee that reported on 15 March 1809, wrote in praise of Appert's procedure, saying that now anybody could use any glass bottle to make his own preserves.[192]

Later in July 1810, the *Gazette de la santé* dedicated a very long article to Nicolas, in somewhat dense prose, in which his discovery is considered by M. Marie de Saint-Ursin to be:

... infinitely useful to trade, medicine, navigation, military hygiene, to establish relations with the colonies... [This process] allows us to offer sailors tired from a long voyage, to the soldiers harassed after a forced march, a healthy meat dish, a consummate restaurant, while experience has shown how animals languish on board ship, and how the operations of a large army prevented it from responding to such embarrassment...[193]

On 22 August 1810, the Secretary of the Society of Agriculture, Commerce, Science and Art, M. Vanzut, followed up the appeal of 21 June 1809 for information that might lead to establishing the art of preserving food. He reported to a public meeting in Châlons-sur-Marne, in the town hall just a short distance from where Nicolas grew up:

The Society has aimed to find all the necessary means for preserving foods. Meanwhile, M. Appert, a Factory Owner at Massy in the Department of Seine-et-Oise, has published, by order of His Excellency the Minister of the Interior, the results of his own work on this important subject. The approval that the Advisory Board of Arts and Manufacturing has given to this work and the award that the Interior Minister has given to M. Appert are a certain guarantee of the usefulness of his discovery. It also gives reason to believe that the problem, the researching of which was the Society's task, is close to being resolved, if not already done so completely. However, starting from the point where M. Appert stopped, it may be useful to look, by new experiments, for ways to link with the destructive principle that nature has attached to all that she has created.[194]

The 6,000 copies of the first edition of "The Book of All Households" were selling well. Nicolas, however, faced some problems with being recognized as the inventor of his procedures. One enterprising Frenchman, by the name of either M. Girard or Gérard, managed to cross the Channel to England, in spite of the naval blockade, and took news of the invention with him. Nicolas wrote that "one Frenchman, M. Girard, a lamp manufacturer, having obtained my book, went to England where he had the effrontery to say he was the inventor of the procedures."[195] This was almost certainly Philippe de Girard, an engineer and inventor. He had made improvements in the design of lamps a few years prior to this date, and so could be called "a lamp manufacturer."

It does not seem that this attempted deception achieved any success for the Frenchman, but it motivated the Englishman Peter Durand, a merchant from "Hoxton Square, in the County of Middlesex, Merchant" to seek and be granted a patent, number 3372 of August 1810, by King George III to:

> make, use, exercise and vend, within England, Wales and the Town of Berwick-upon-Tweed, an invention communicated to him by a certain foreigner residing abroad, of the method of "Preserving animal food, vegetable food, and other perishable articles a long time from perishing or becoming useless."

The patent then outlines Nicolas's method but including, for the first time, tin vessels:

> First, I place and enclose the said food or articles in bottles or other vessels of glass, pottery, tin or other metals or fit materials; and I do close the aperture of such containing vessels so as completely to cut off and exclude all communication with the external air; and as to the method of closing, I do avail myself of the usual means of corking, airing, luting, or cementing, and in large vessels I make use of corks formed of pieces glued together in such a manner as that the pores of that substance shall be in a cross direction with regard to the aperture into which such corks are to be driven; and I do also in such vessels as may admit of or require the same, make use of stoppers fitted or ground with emery, or screw caps with or without a ring of leather, or other soft substance between the faces of closure, and also of corks or cross plugs or covers of

leather, cloth, parchment, bladder, and the like.

Secondly, when the vessels have been thus charged and well closed, I do place them in a boiler, each separately surrounded with straw or wrapped in coarse cloth, or otherwise defended from striking against each other, and I fill the said boiler so as to cover the vessels with cold water, which I gradually heat to boiling, and continue the ebullition for a certain time, which must depend upon the nature of the substances included in the vessels, and the size of the said vessels, and other obvious circumstances which will be easily apprehended by the operator without farther instruction. Vegetable substances are to be put into the vessel in the raw or crude state, and animal substances partly or half cooked, although these may also be put in raw. The food or other articles thus prepared may be kept for a very long time in a state fit for use, care being taken that the vessel shall not be opened until their said contents shall be wanted for consumption.

And, lastly, I do declare, that although the application of the water bath, as herein-before described, may be the most commodious and convenient, I do likewise avail myself of the application of heat by placing the said vessels in an oven, or a stove, or a steam bath, or any other fit situation for gradually and uniformly raising the temperature of the same, and suffering them to cool again; and farther, that I do, as the choice of the consumer or the nature of the said food or other article may render preferable, leave the aperture of the vessel, or a small proportion thereof, open until the effect of the heat shall have taken place, at which period I close the same.

Durand finished his application:

In witness whereof, I, the said Peter Durand, have hereunto set my hand and seal, the Thirtieth day of August, in the year of our Lord One thousand eight hundred and ten.
    Peter Durand

And be it remembered, that on the Thirtieth Day of August in the year of our Lord 1810, the aforesaid Peter Durand came before our said Lord, the King in His Chancery, and acknowledged the Specification aforesaid, and all and everything therein contained and specified, in form above written. And also the Specification aforesaid was stamped according to the tenor of the Statute made for that purpose.

Enrolled the Thirtieth day of August, in the year of our Lord One thousand eight hundred and ten. [196]

Peter Durand stated that he had carried out a variety of experiments to preserve various foods in large quantities, using "tin cases." In an approach similar to Nicolas's, Durand submitted his preserved food to the Royal Society, under the Presidency of Sir Joseph Banks, and the Royal Institution. The various tests were successful, including food that had been on board ship for four months.[197]

In spite of the progress he had been able to make, Peter Durand decided not to go into production himself, but instead sold his patent rights in 1812 to Bryan Donkin and John Hall for £1,000.[198] Donkin and Hall set up the first canning factory to use tin cans in 1813, in Blue Anchor Road, Bermondsey in south-east London.

Meanwhile, back in France, the *Gazette Nationale ou Le Moniteur Universel*, often just known as the *Moniteur*, published a long article about Nicolas's book on 1 September 1810. This newspaper had first been published on 24 November 1789 by Charles-Joseph Panckoucke, and had rapidly become the major newspaper of the Revolution. Napoleon later declared it the government's official newspaper in 1799. The article said:

This art, which concerns both our needs and our pleasures, has been the subject of past research and discovery more or less successful, of which the application was more or less easy. Among the modern scholars, and probably the ancients too, no-one has carried the talent of preserving food as far as M. Appert.... He is associated by this with the glory and general recognition which are due to one of the most useful of our philanthropists.[199]

Meanwhile, Nicolas's book was translated into German by Charles Mohr, the chief pharmacist of the General Hospital in Koblenz. Herr Mohr sent a copy of the translation to the Minister of the Interior and another to Nicolas. Since Nicolas spent three years in the Rhineland Palatinate as a catering cadet in the ducal court of Christian IV, he might well have been able to appreciate the translation. The German edition was published in October 1810 by *Pauli und comp.* of Koblenz.

In his book, Nicolas had made it clear that he did not know the reasons behind the success of his method. In an important passage, he shows that he knew the limits of his understanding, and as a true scientist he did not take to himself more credit than he could feel justified by his years of experimental work:

Not to my knowledge has any author, ancient or modern, indicated, nor even surmised, the principle that forms the basis of the method which I offer...

It is due to my experiments, in which I have persevered, that I am convinced that heat has the essential quality in itself not only of changing the combination of the constituent parts of animal and vegetable products, but also, if not destroying, at least of arresting for many years the natural tendency of these same products to decomposition. In addition I am convinced that its application in a proper manner to all these products, after having deprived them in the most rigorous manner possible of contact with the air, effects perfect preservation of these same products with all their natural qualities.

At first sight, one might think that a substance, either raw or prepared on the fire, then bottled in a vacuum and completely sealed, would also be preserved without the application of heat in a water bath; this would be a mistake.[200]

Nicolas's summary is a more accurate view of the reality behind his method than that of the renowned Joseph Louis Gay-Lussac. Following the latter's involvement in the committee that investigated Nicolas's methods, he read a paper to the *Institut de France* on 3 December 1810 endeavouring to give a scientific basis to the process. This was published in the Annals of Chemistry on 31 December 1810. He stated:

> Vegetable or animal substances, through their contact with air, acquire immediately a disposition to putrefaction or fermentation; but in exposing them to the temperature of boiling water in well closed vessels, the absorbed oxygen produces a new combination, which is no longer able to excite fermentation or putrefaction, when it becomes solid by heat in the same way as albumen... One can conclude also that the reason it is preserved for a long time without fermentation is because the outside surface does not yield to oxygen. This proves that the fermentation cannot start without the help of oxygen.[201]

Many years later, Louis Pasteur gave the scientific explanation of Appert's method. He showed that what was occurring was the destruction by heat of germs; these germs were contained in the air and the food. Therefore the oxygen itself was not the cause of the problems with food, and so oxygen had no influence on Appert's procedure, contrary to Gay-Lussac's belief.

A second, revised and augmented, edition of Nicolas's book was issued in 1811, with a print run of 4,000 copies. This was closely followed by a third edition in 1813.

There was then a gap until a fourth edition, like the previous two revised and enlarged by Nicolas, in 1831. Following Nicolas's death, a fifth edition, published in 1852, was edited by his nephew M. Prieur-Appert and M. Gannal.

The first translation of Nicolas's book was the German

edition mentioned above, published in 1810. There was another German edition in 1822. A Swedish edition appeared in 1811. The first of the English editions appeared in late 1811, published by Black, Perry and Kingsbury, Booksellers to the Hon. East India Company, Leadenhall Street, London.[202] There was a second version of this translation in 1812, together with an American version of this translation the same year. A Belgian edition was published in 1821.

In 1920 a further English translation of the 1810 French edition appeared, translated by Katherine Golden Bitting, who also wrote a short biographical tribute to Nicolas, *Un bienfaiteur de l'humanité*, a title possibly bestowed on Nicolas in 1822. K. G Bitting also translated the fourth French edition into English, which was published in 1921.

Nicolas concluded his 1810 first edition of his book with a description, as he could then envisage it, of the benefits of his methods:

No one will doubt, after all the experiments I have detailed, that the adoption of this new method, which, as may be seen, unites the greatest economy to a perfection unlooked for until the present time, will secure the following advantages.

1. That of considerably diminishing the consumption of sugar, the produce of the cane, and of giving the greatest extension to the manufactories of grape syrup.

2. That of preserving for use in all countries and all seasons, a number of alimentary and medicinal productions, which being very abundant in some places at certain seasons, are therefore wasted, being considered as of no value; while the same substances, under other circumstances, being much wanted, become of double or even four-fold value; and sometimes cannot be procured at any price, such as butter and eggs.

3. That of procuring for civil and military hospitals, and even for the armies the most valuable assistance, the details of which would be superfluous here. But the great advantage of this

method consists principally in its application to the service of the Navy. It will supply fresh and wholesome provisions for his majesty's vessels on long voyages with a saving of more than fifty per cent. Mariners will in case of illness be furnished with broth, various and cooling beverages, vegetables and fruits; in a word, they will be able to partake of a number of alimentary and medicinal substances, which will alone be sufficient to prevent or cure the diseases contracted at sea, more especially the worst of them all, scurvy. These advantages eminently merit the public attention when we reflect that salted provisions, and above all their bad qualities, have caused the loss of more lives at sea than shipwrecks and naval engagements.

4. Medicine will find in this method the means of relieving humanity, by the facility of meeting everywhere and in all seasons, animal substances and all kinds of vegetables, as well as their juices, preserved with all their natural qualities and virtues: by the same means it will obtain resources infinitely precious in the production of distant regions, preserved in their fresh state.

5. From this method will arise a new branch of industry, relative to the productions of France, by their circulation through the interior, and the exportation abroad, of the produce with which nature has blessed the different countries.

6. This method will facilitate the exportation of the wine of many vineyards: wine which can scarcely be kept a year, even when not removed from the spot, may hereafter be preserved many years though sent abroad.

Finally, this invention cannot fail to enlarge the domain of Chymistry (sic), and become the common benefit of all countries, which will derive the most precious fruit from it.

So many advantages, and an infinity of others which the imagination of the reader will easily conceive, produced by one and the same cause, are a source of astonishment.[203]

J. Roulleau, sculpteur

NICOLAS
APPERT

Commemorative First Day Cover Postcard
5 March 1955
See the photograph on the following page

(From the author's collection)

Bust of Nicolas Appert
c1892
by Jules-Pierre Roulleau (1855 – 1895)

Photograph by the author taken at the *Musée Schiller et Goethe*,
Châlons-en-Champagne, in 2008

Chapter 9

Disaster in Massy: 1811 – 1816

In May 1811, Nicolas wrote to the Minister of the Interior asking for permission to run a course of practical tuition of his methods of preserving foods at the School of Pharmacy in Paris. Permission was granted and so inventor turned teacher as he led his students through his procedures.[204]

Nicolas was honoured in *L'Almanach des Gourmands*, eighth edition in 1812, by being included in a poem praising those who delighted the palate of the "Gourmands." Entitled *Poésies Gourmandes*, in the sixth stanza Nicolas appears:

> One improvises a hymn affable
> In honour of the famous Appert,
> Everywhere so commendable,
> Of his state the great expert
> With discoveries so admirable
> Peerless mortal we assert.[205]

The poem continues for many lines celebrating the variety of foods that Appert has enabled Gourmands to enjoy at times of the year when previously it would have been impossible. It concludes, a little verbosely, with:

> To immortalise him, sing,
> As a poet and as a friend,
> Of his great learning,
> And no less brilliant

147

In surpassing Ghent
In the art of patisserie, illustrating
Better than my words, how much praised
Because of his duck pâté,
And since many a celebrity,
Honourably cited,
From Amiens to Provence,
Throughout the Empire and even outside France,
By all gourmets, are delighted
In his good taste, and in his science.

Elsewhere in the same volume, Grimod de la Reynière wrote that since M. Appert had divulged his great secret many had tried to make similar preparations. However, "as it takes a lot of skill, patience and practice to succeed, few people" had achieved them. Consequently, Appert's stores were as busy as ever, in fact so much so that stocks had begun to dwindle, making it difficult to purchase them in the winter.[206]

Meanwhile, Nicolas continued to have problems with people either misrepresenting his work, or attributing it to others. In the 1812 Yearbook of French Industry, a contributor, Arsenne Thiébault de Berneaud, a well-known botanist and writer of scientific pamphlets, said that Appert's method consisted of destroying the "ferments of substances, and then enclosing them in a box to protect them from air." In the 1813 third edition of his book, Nicolas corrected this view: the "ferments" were to be destroyed while in a hermetically sealed vessel, not prior to being enclosed.[207]

Other theories were put forward. In the April 1812 Journal of the Rural and Domestic Economy, Issue 109, Nicolas's invention was attributed to the Reverend Georg Eisen von Schwarzenberg, of Torma in Livonia, in the present day Baltic state of Estonia. Eisen was indeed an inventor: for example, he is known for creating a popular hair powder out of potato starch. The Journal article not only ascribed the invention of preserved food to the wrong person, it also repeated Arsenne Thiébault de Berneaud's incorrect description of Nicolas's method. Nicolas's reaction was: "I am angry and upset for the Journal's readers!"[208]

Nicolas produced his longest reaction – fifteen pages in his book – to demonstrate the differences between his own method and that of another author, M. Cadet Devaux. The latter had produced a book, *Le Ménage des fruits,* which thus had a similar title to Nicolas's *Le Livre de Tous Les Ménages*. Nicolas reported that many had bought Cadet Devaux's book in error when intending to buy his. Unusually for Nicolas, he did not take this to be a personal attack, but rather was able to contrast what to a large extent he considered to be complementary methods. He could not, however, manage other than to imply that his own methods were both perfected and superior, and that he would be happy to help Cadet Devaux improve his methods.[209]

Nicolas's financial problems now seemed to be behind him. Although his book only brought him a fraction of the money that a patent would have, he was able, in September 1812, to repay money that he had borrowed from a M. Trubert in 1806, at the time of the Appert bankruptcy.[210]

By the middle of September 1812, the huge French Army had advanced as far as Moscow, capturing the almost deserted city, but not defeating the Russian army or bringing Tsar Alexander I to submission. Napoleon's fortunes were turning, and with the retreat in the bitter winter, the French Army fell to less than a tenth of its original size. By May 1813 Napoleon was again on the offensive, inflicting defeats on Prussia and Russia at Lützen near Leipzig, where both sides lost about 20,000 men, and then 18 days later and 115 miles away at Bautzen, beyond Dresden. Here too, losses amounted to about 20,000 on each side.

There was a brief truce (the Armistice of Pleischwitz)

from 4 June until 16 August 1813: both sides had suffered about a quarter of a million casualties since April. The main result, however, was that an Austrian army also took to the field, joining Napoleon's enemies, when the armistice ended. Napoleon was now outnumbered in Germany by two to one.

A huge force of Austrians, Prussians and Russians brought Napoleon to battle at Dresden on Thursday 26 August 1813, only to be defeated once more by the French Emperor. In October, however, Napoleon was forced to retreat back to France after his decisive defeat at the Battle of the Nations near Leipzig. This, the largest battle in Europe before World War I, involved around half a million troops. The French were steadily beaten back, first across the Rhine, and then deeper into France. Napoleon's army of around 100,000 men now faced more than five times as many in the large coalition ranged against him.

In March 1814 Napoleon won several battles against enemy forces as they advanced towards Paris, but none were decisive. Just before the coalition against Napoleon entered Paris on 31 March 1814, the war came to Massy.

Around 25 March 1814, the Prussians arrived at Massy and seized Nicolas's factory and his house for their injured. They set up a field hospital there, destroying everything in the workshop that got in their way and using furniture and anything else that could burn for fires. Nicolas and his family took to the barn for their living quarters. Their fields and crops, their buildings and belongings, all were ransacked or destroyed, leaving everything devastated when finally the field hospital was moved to Paris.[211]

Nicolas, Elisabeth and their family took temporary refuge in Paris, possibly at Nicolas's general warehouse at *N° 14 rue du Marché des Jacobins*. This was a fruiterer and merchant store run by M. Malliez.[212] At least sales could continue there, while stocks lasted.

Following Napoleon's abdication on Wednesday 6 April 1814, and the Treaty of Fontainebleau five days later, life began slowly to get back to normal. Returning to Massy, Nicolas faced the prospect of rebuilding his factory.

While Napoleon was escorted to his exile at Elba, a small island off the coast of Italy, Louis XVIII became King of France. The new regime refused to honour the debts of Napoleon's government, which would have greatly affected Nicolas as he had been owed a considerable sum by the Maritime department.

As well as having to rebuild his factory and await the next harvest for the goods to preserve, Nicolas was concerned about two other things. He wanted to be recognised as the inventor of his procedures – especially in England, since the false report by Girard/Gérard, who had claimed to be the inventor. He was also very keen to see the canning using tinplate rather than bottles.

So, incredibly, just a few weeks after the devastation of his factory at Massy, Nicolas set sail for England. For the first time in his life, he crossed a sea and arrived in Dover in June 1814. Nicolas took with him various samples of his products, with a certificate signed by M. Bouriat giving the date they were preserved.[213]

Nicolas met with a committee of six English scientists from the ranks of the Royal Society:

Sir Joseph Banks PRS (1743 – 1820):
> botanist, naturalist and explorer – he had taken part in Captain Cook's first great voyage. Sir Joseph was President of the Royal Society from 1778 until his death in 1820, and so was in that position at the time of Nicolas's visit

Sir Charles Blagden FRS (1748 – 1820):
> physician and scientist, author of Blagden's Law which states that the freezing point of a solution decreases in

direct proportion to the concentration of the solution

William Hyde Wollaston MD FRS (1766 – 1828)
> chemist and physicist, who discovered the elements palladium in 1803 and rhodium in 1804. He was subsequently President of the Royal Society

Dr John Lewis Tiarks (1789 – 1837)
> mathematician, astronomer, Assistant Librarian to Sir Joseph Banks 1810 – 1816, and from 1817 to 1821 British Astronomer to the American Boundary Commission, made FRS in 1825

J. Loyel
> about whom unfortunately I cannot discover anything!

W. A. Cadell FRS
> scientist, traveller and author.

On Sunday 26 June 1814, Nicolas met with this august committee and they published a short report two days later:

> To M. Appert, author of The Art of Preserving All Kinds of Alimentary Substances:
>
> We, the undersigned, certify that the bottle containing milk, mentioned by the certificate of M. Bouriat, having been unsealed by us on 26 June 1814, we tasted the milk, which was found to be perfectly smooth, free from any sourness, but with a slightly different flavour from fresh milk. The other preserved substances that we tasted at the same time were all in a perfectly preserved state, and appeared to have lost none of their taste.
>
> Signed: Jos. Banks, C. Blagden, W. H. Wollaston, L. Tiarks, J. Loyel, W. A. Cadell

This report was also published in the 1814 bulletin of the *Société d'Encouragement pour l'Industrie Nationale* in Paris.[214]

When Nicolas stopped at a tavern in the City, he found an interesting method being used that gave him pause for thought. He later wrote:

> During my trip to London in 1814 I saw in a tavern in the City, the one where the Bank holds its fêtes, a very simple steam device, and with which is cooked daily dinner for five to six hundred people.[215]

This led Nicolas to plan to increase the size of his pots, and extend the use of steam to heat them.

Meanwhile, the second reason for his journey to England would have led him to a factory south of the Thames, named Donkin and Hall's.

John Hall was born in 1764, the second of four sons of a millwright in Dartford. He established a foundry in Dartford in 1785 that eventually produced steam engines. John Hall was known as a millwright and engineer.

Bryan Donkin was born in Fountain Hall, Sandoe, in Northumbria in 1768, the third son in a family of eight. His father was an agent for the Duke of Northumberland. At first, Donkin trained as a surveyor and then worked as a land agent in Kent. Then in 1792, aged 24, Donkin was apprenticed at John Hall's of Dartford. After 10 years, Donkin left Hall's, and worked for the Fourdrinier brothers, perfecting a paper milling machine. Donkin went with Hall's blessing, and £250 to start his workshop, plus the hand in marriage of Hall's wife's sister Mary Brome.

Donkin established his workshop at Fort Place, Blue Anchor Road, Bermondsey. The Fourdrinier brothers poured such great quantities of cash into the project that they were finally declared bankrupt in 1810. Donkin, however, continued to thrive, becoming the leading European paper manufacturer.

When Peter Durand offered his Patent for preserving food

in tin containers for sale, Bryan Donkin and John Hall bought it and went into partnership at Bermondsey to produce preserved food in tin canisters, or cans. They started production in 1811, but lost a great deal of money in their early days.[216] However, by 1812 they were supplying the Royal Navy.

All cans were made by hand and filled through a hole in the top or side, which was then soldered. The can was opened with a chisel and hammer. The can opener was not invented until 1858.

The visit to Donkin & Hall's factory must have given Nicolas a great deal to think about. He was aware that English tin was of a much higher quality than anything he could get in France. He would not only have to put his preserves in tin cans rather than glass bottles, but would also have to manufacture the tin can in the first place.

Nicolas returned to Massy and no doubt laid ambitious plans. Unfortunately he did not have the opportunity to carry them out. Napoleon escaped from Elba, arriving in France on Wednesday 1 March 1815. By the 20th he was in Paris.

Between these two dates, on Thursday 16 March 1815, Nicolas and Elisabeth's fourth child, Amélie-Justine, married Jean-Louis Lefébure. The marriage took place at the Appert home in Massy, with both of the bride's parents signing the marriage register. Amélie-Justine was 21 years old; her new husband was exactly one month older.[217] Jean-Louis's parents, Jean and Marie Lefébure, had run a haberdashery store in Paris until Jean's death just over a year before. At that point, no doubt Jean-Louis, although only 20 years old, would have taken over the running of the business with his mother.

Jean-Louis and Amélie-Justine lived at *Nᵒ 13 rue du Coq, St. Honoré*, in Paris. This was the Lefébure family home, where Jean-Louis had grown up, behind or very near their store.

Four days after the family wedding at Massy, Napoleon arrived in Paris. He managed to recruit an army of over a third of a million, and ruled for his Hundred Days. The coalition again mobilised against Napoleon and, of course, final defeat came at the hands of the Duke of Wellington and von Blücher of Prussia at Waterloo, in present day Belgium, on Sunday 18 June 1815.

With what can only be considered immense bad luck, Nicolas and Elisabeth's property at Massy was again ransacked following a Napoleonic defeat. This time, it was the turn of the English to be the culprits. Looking back, Nicolas wrote in his 1831 book:

> At the time of the second invasion, when the allies had destroyed from top to bottom my beautiful establishment at Massy that they had transformed into a hospital, I took refuge in Paris with a few remnants of my appliances.[218]

In 1825 Nicolas described the events in a letter:

> In 1815, the English made my house into a hospital, which ruined me to the point that, having been forced to borrow because of the occupation, I had to sell the remnants of my equipment to live in reduced circumstances in the *rue Cassette* in Paris.[219]

The Appert family moved into *N° 17 rue Cassette* in the *faubourg Saint-Germain*, about a kilometre south west of the *Île de la Cité*. Nicolas was unable to continue with any of his work, whether preserving food or carrying out his beloved experiments.

On Saturday 4 May 1816, Nicolas sold off his property in Massy. It was so large that it was divided into sixteen lots for sale. Nicolas was able to pay off the mortgage on the property fully with the proceeds of the sale, and even managed to reimburse some of his many creditors.[220]

Above and Opposite:
Nicolas Appert lived at *N° 17 rue Cassette*
from 1815 to 1817

Nicolas, Elisabeth and their family had been at Massy since November 1802. So much had happened in the last fourteen years. Nicolas had gambled on opening a factory, growing and bottling his own food. He had gone bankrupt, but recovered with his preserves winning accolades from the Parisian society leaders, the Navy, the Society for the Encouragement of National Industry, and many local newspapers and journals. He had even become the author of a bestselling book that was already being translated around Europe and in the United States of America. Then war had come to Massy and devasted his prospects – twice. Nicolas, at the age of 66, had to begin to make his fortune again. He was back in Paris, as he had been in 1784, half his life ago, full of ideas and enterprise.

In spite of the bad experiences in Massy, he was to live there again. He would, in fact, eventually die and be buried there.

At its meeting on Wednesday 6 November 1816, the Society for the Encouragement of National Industry decided to award medals to notable inventors. In its first award, it presented Nicolas with a silver medal:

> To M. Appert, for employing for the preservation of meat, fish, fruit, vegetables, butter and milk, a simple process, the application to these various foodstuffs being new, the success of which was recognized even abroad, which can be, at least by the promise of this example, of great usefulness, even though the inventor has not achieved in practice all the developments that were hoped for: a silver medal.[221]

However, for a man of Nicolas's stature, this was almost an indignity. The silver medal placed him in the second rank of inventors, not among the greatest. The Society presented gold medals to M. Raymond, a chemistry professor from Lyons, for having "devised a strong new blue colour that gives pleasant shades to silk" and to M. Allard "inventor of a shimmering metallic varnish."

The Society followed up this first prize award at the same meeting by setting out a programme of awards for the following three years, including this one:

> Committee of the Economic Arts: A prize of 2,000 *francs*, proposed for 1818 for the preservation of food through M. Appert's process, executed on a larger scale, or by any similar method.

Without doubt, Nicolas would have dearly loved to have been in a position to achieve this award. However, as he later wrote:

> This same year 1816, the Society for the Encouragement of National Industry awarded me a silver medal, and proposed a prize of 2,000 *francs* to anyone who could form an establishment to preserve meat in large tinned plate containers, containing up to eight or ten kilograms of boned beef.
>
> Several of the most eminent members of this Society invited me to compete for this prize, but, totally ruined, it was impossible for me to get the funds and the premises with

enough space to conduct this business.[222]

On 12 March 1817, encouraged by some of the members of the Society, Nicolas applied to the Minister of the Interior for a grant of some premises.[223] It would take five months before the wheels of the state would turn sufficiently for there to be a decision.

Meanwhile, Nicolas sent a brief report to the Society for their meeting on Wednesday 9 April 1817. In the report, Nicolas recommends that the government take on the responsibility for creating an establishment that would achieve the preservation of food on a large scale.[224]

Then on Friday 8 August 1817, Nicolas received an offer from the Minister of the Interior, Joseph Vicomte Lainé, which was probably beyond anything he could have hoped for. The government proposed that Nicolas take over premises of some 4,000 m^2, with the state paying the annual rent of 4,000 *francs*.[225] The new Appert factory was to be installed at *N° 17 rue Moreau*, in the *faubourg Sainte-Antoine*, just across the River Seine from the *rue Cassette*.

Nicolas's new premises were to be in part of the Hospital of the "Fifteen-Twenties": *l'hospice des Quinze-Vingts*.

L'hospice des Quinze-Vingts

Above: From an old postcard[226]

Below: All that remains, at *N° 28 rue de Charenton, Paris*

Chapter 10

At *l'hospice des Quinze-Vingts*, Paris
1817 – 1827

In 1260 King Louis IX, later to be canonised as St. Louis, founded the hospital known as *Quinze-Vingts* to take care of soldiers blinded during the Seventh Crusade.

The wonderful name of the hospital is from the *système vicésimal*, based on the number 20, which was in common use in the Europe of the Early Middle Ages. The counting system in France still has a remnant of this in the use of *quatre-vingts* for 80. Literally then, *Quinze-Vingts* equalled 15 x 20, and so 300. This stood for the number of beds for the blind that the hospital contained.

The hospital moved in 1780 from its original site on the *rue Saint-Honoré* to *N° 28 rue de Charenton*. This new location had previously been the barracks of a squadron of the Queen's Black Musketeers (so called because they rode black horses), who had been disbanded by Louis XVI in 1775. Now a research and medical centre, *Le Centre Hospitalier National d'Ophtalmologie des Quinze-Vingts* is still located in the same building, fully rebuilt except for the entrance porch to the musketeers' chapel and barracks (shown opposite).

The *rue de Charenton* is one of the radial roads leading from the *place de la Bastille*. The *Quinze-Vingts* was built fronting onto the *rue de Charenton* and with the *rue Moreau* at the side furthest from the Bastille. Nicolas moved into these extremely spacious premises in 1817.

The lease on the property had been taken out by the then Director-General of Commerce and Manufacturing, Jean Antoine Chaptal, *comte Chaptal de Chanteloup*, in May 1815, during Napoleon's Hundred Days. Chaptal had been a co-founder of the *Société d'Encouragement pour l'Industrie Nationale,* together with *Le baron* Louis-Jacques Thénard and Jean Baptiste André Dumas, on 2 November 1801. The government undertook to pay the rent until the end of the lease in June 1824.

Known as the *enclos des Mousquetaires*, number 17 had extensive accommodation. There was a large building at the end of the second courtyard of the hospice. On the ground floor there were at least six rooms. There was a very large open area, a large square room, two workshop areas, a small office, and a small store-room. A staircase led down to a basement that contained six further work rooms, three of which had a fireplace, and three offices on the other side of the stairs, of which two had fireplaces. The first floor was split into four very large rooms.

There was a small stable outside built against the boundary wall, with a cellar below. There were two further outside workshops, plus a latrine block in the third courtyard. Responsibility for annual emptying of the pit latrines lay with the landlord, except for at the end of the lease when the lease-holder had to empty them!

Although 67 years of age, Nicolas set to work to fit out these new premises both for production of Appert preserves and for research into improvements of the process. As early as 15 September 1817, production began at *N° 17 rue Moreau*, although doubtless not very much of the premises had been transformed by that time.[227]

Nicolas later explained that he spent more than 30,000 *francs* on the instruments and furnishings needed for the business. He wrote to the Minister of the Interior: "Since that time, *Monseigneur*, I have not recouped my losses, but have lived, rendering service to the State and its navy, and in training students, while also perfecting my processes in several ways."[228]

At this time Nicolas produced as much as he could to provision a long voyage. Captain Louis-Claude de Saulces de Freycinet and his distinguished crew circumnavigated the globe in the corvette *L'Uranie*. The ship departed from Toulon on the south coast of France on 17 September 1817. They took with them a large supply of Appert preserves, returning in November 1820. We shall meet the Captain upon his return, at which time he gave testimony to the excellence of the food that Appert provided.

The aims of Captain de Freycinet's voyage were primarily scientific. Throughout their journey they took readings of the strength of the earth's magnetic field. They surveyed the location of a great number of islands, especially in the Pacific. The Captain and his crew collected a large number of flora and fauna specimens, and their investigations covered geology, mineralogy, hydrography and astronomy. De Freycinet was secretly accompanied by his wife, Rose, who was disguised as a midshipman for the first leg of their journey. Rose therefore became the first white woman to land in Western Australia and to see many Pacific islands.

There are several records of the journey. "The Asiatic Journal and Monthly Register for British India and its Dependencies" for January to June 1821 carried an account in English based on a previous publication in *Le Moniteur*. This was reproduced, and slightly embellished, in Captain Samuel Prior's 1840 book "All the Voyages round the World from the first by Magellan, in 1520, to that of de Freycinet, in 1820." However, for the serious student, de Freycinet himself wrote a 13 volume account, together with 4 atlases, with the lengthy title *Voyage autour du monde fait par ordre du Roi, sur les corvettes Uranie et la Physicienne, pendant les années 1817, 1818, 1819 et 1820.*

De Freycinet was not the only one of those who took part in the voyage to produce an account. Draughtsman to the expedition, Jacques Etienne Victor Arago, improved on the length of de Freycinet's title. He wrote "Narrative of a voyage around the world in the Uranie and Physicienne corvettes commanded by Captain de Freycinet during the years 1817, 1818, 1819 and 1820, on a scientific expedition undertaken by order of the French government in a series of letters to a friend." This was published in 1823.

Each of these continued to keep the secret of Rose de Freycinet's presence, until her journal of the voyage - *Campagne de l'Uranie (1817–1820)* – which was published after she died in 1832. An English translation of her journal "A Woman of Courage: The Journal of Rose de Freycinet on her Voyage around the World 1817-1820" by Marc Serge Rivière was first published in 1996.

The voyage had nearly ended in disaster as they were shipwrecked in the Falkland Islands, losing their ship *l'Uranie* and about half of their collected specimens. They were rescued by an American whaler, which de Freycinet purchased and renamed *La Physicienne*.

Meanwhile, back in Paris, Elisabeth and Nicolas became grandparents. However, the arrival of their grandchild was not as happy an event for them as might have been expected. Their daughter Aglaë-Françoise, aged 29 in 1818, became an unmarried mother. Aglaë's daughter, Athenaïs Louisa Joséphine, was born on Monday 29 June 1818. This may have led to an estrangement between parents and daughter. When Aglaë-Françoise died ten years later she left her daughter to the care of Joseph Marie Barbieri, who had recognised Athenaïs as his child at the time of her birth.[229]

Meanwhile, Nicolas continued to be the subject of articles about his processes. In late October, this article appeared in the Annals of French Agriculture, 1818, giving Nicolas the new title of *Conservateur Universel*:

> The food preparations of M. Appert are now too generally known and appreciated for it to be necessary to emphasise their immeasurable usefulness; and it is right that the gastronomes of Europe have agreed to give him the title of *"Conservateur Universel."*
>
> Who in fact better deserves this name, than the resourceful and hard-working genius who, successfully applying chemistry to the culinary art, has managed to preserve throughout the flavour and integrity of every animal and vegetable substance that is good for the nourishment of mankind? In a less enlightened century than ours, M. Appert would have been charged as a sorcerer, or taken before the Holy Inquisition; for it would have been impossible to consider him otherwise than as a professor of the occult sciences, that man could succeed in eating fresh food in Peking, or to serve in Constantinople, St. Petersburg or in Pondicherry, a complete dinner prepared in the *faubourg St. Antoine*.
>
> But far from abusing these discoveries and deceiving men, M. Appert has, on the contrary, placed the public in his confidence and given them the fruits of his genius and long experience.
>
> In his book entitled "The Book For All Households" he has revealed without mystery all his secrets and has put each of his readers in reach of preserving for himself the fruit of his orchard, the vegetables of his garden and the products of his farmyard.[230]

The article also described how, following the destruction of his factory at Massy by the allied armies, the government had provided him with premises at *Quinze-Vingts*. There, it informed its readers, M. Appert was embarking on a new phase of his research – to preserve up to 15 lbs of beef in tin cans.

On Wednesday 24 March 1819, at the meeting of the Society for the Encouragement of National Industry, a new word was coined: *appertisation*.[231] The meeting was devoted to the use of the metal can in Nicolas's processes and Denis-Placide Bouriat presented the formal report:

Gentlemen, I have had the honour of bringing before you, these ten years, processes employed by M. Appert to preserve meat and vegetables. My report, receiving your approval, was very helpful to this artist, for it influenced the Government to grant him special protection. However, I did not ignore the fact that his processes, good in themselves, would become more advantageous if we replaced, by other less fragile vessels, the glass bottles which M. Appert uses. He appreciated the importance of this observation and resolved to apply it as soon as his capacities permitted. He was outstripped by a neighbouring nation which knows so well how to take advantage of valuable discoveries, wherever they arise.

Therefore, it was in England that meat first began to be preserved in tin cans...

Visiting the workshops of M. Appert, we saw the means he employs. They are in all respects similar to those we have just indicated which are practised in England ... He has asked us to try two of his cans, one of which contained veal, chicken and beef, and the other four partridges, announcing that they were in his shop for the last three months. We have waited a further two months before opening them.

This took place here in the presence of several members of various committees. The partridge had the flavour and aroma they enjoyed when they were put into the can...

M. Appert furnishes abroad, to our colonies, specialities of France whose qualities are superior to those grown elsewhere. Thus different peoples enjoy a range of delicacies such as turkeys with truffles, red partridges, quail, *pâté de foie gras*, and so on. The people of France can extend throughout the year enjoyment that at the moment can be enjoyed by them for only one season.

Commemorative First Day Cover Postcard
by Henry Lucien Cheffer (1888 – 1957)
5 March 1955

(From the author's collection)

Finally, with time and improvements, we hope to see realised the idea that we put forward: that all countries in the world could enjoy the products that are specific to each one of them, and in this respect, France, which has the least to desire and most to offer, can only gain from this exchange.

Already, in consulting the price list of meat preserved in London and the one printed by M. Appert, one sees an opportunity in our favour: he offers at 1 *franc* 75 *centimes* that which sells for 3 *francs* in England. He has even assured us that by working in large amounts of the meat of large animals, like beef and veal, he could set the price at 1 *franc* 25 *centimes* a half-kilogram, with no bones, but the weight of the vessel included.

Based on these considerations, our Committee of Economic Arts offers to publicize this method of preservation and encourage consumers to use these products.[232]

In early 1820 stirrings continued against the Bourbon Restoration under Louis XVIII. The King's nephew, Charles-Ferdinand *duc de Berry*, was stabbed with a seven-inch dagger driven into his breast up to the hilt, outside the Paris Opera on the evening of 13 February. The assassin, Louis-Pierre Louvel, aged 37, was a devoted Bonapartist. He had followed Napoleon into exile in Elba, working in his stables as a saddler, and had been in his army throughout the Hundred Days when Napoleon had returned to power up to and including the defeat at Waterloo. Since then it seemed that he had been laying plans to make the restored monarchy pay for Napoleon's defeat and final exile. His victim was the only male in the Bourbon line likely to produce an heir: by eliminating him there would be no Bourbon successor. The *duc de Berry* did, however, produce an heir: a posthumous son, Henri, *duc de Bordeaux*, was born seven months later on 29 September.

On 3 April 1820 Nicolas and Elisabeth's daughter Aglaë-Françoise had another child. This grandson, Achille-Jean-Baptiste Alexis, did not survive into adulthood.[233] By the time of his mother's death in 1828, aged 39, Achille had already died. In 1820, Aglaë-Françoise was still unmarried and living in Paris. Possibly any family rift had by now become permanent. Nicolas and Elisabeth may not even have known of their grandson's birth.

By the summer of 1820, Nicolas had been in the *Quinze-Vingts* premises for three years, and production was running at between 1,200 and 1,500 tins per month. He still produced his preserves in glass bottles as well, as he could not obtain sufficient good quality tins to keep up with demand. The superiority of English tin had meanwhile enabled Donkin's of London to produce tins weighing in excess of 5kg.

Meanwhile, Nicolas had his sights firmly set on the award of a gold medal and the 2,000 *francs* that the *Société d'Encouragement pour l'Industrie Nationale* had offered, with a deadline for contributions of 1 July 1820. In order to be eligible he had to present a large tin – of at least 8kg – of preserved meat. Nicolas produced a tin weighing 10kg, but unfortunately when the committee removed the bones from the beef, it weighed just 6.25kg.

Nicolas found himself competing for the gold medal against an old acquaintance. Back in January 1806, as part of his long journey to visit all his retailers, he had met M. Quinton in Bordeaux and very probably instructed him in his processes. No doubt they continued their discussions by correspondence. Quinton had set up his own factory at *N° 71 cours du Jardin-Public* in Bordeaux. Quinton's cans also did not achieve the 8kg requirement – his heaviest was 5kg.

When the Society met on 6 September 1820 to announce its verdicts, it awarded a Gold Medal to both Nicolas and M. Quinton.[234] Unlike the Silver awarded to Nicolas four years before, this was no insult. This placed him in the first rank of French scientists. The only disappointment was that the Society decided not to award the prize of 2,000 *francs* since no-one had actually achieved the required 8kg weight. At the same meeting, the Society decided to define again what would satisfy them:

> A new prize is proposed of 2,000 F for the person who forms an establishment in which, employing any procedure, one can preserve, for more than a year, animal and vegetable substances in a fresh state or of recent preparation, with an actual weight of at least 8 or 10kg in one vessel.

Although the Society set the date of July 1821 for the award, an absence of candidates led to their renewing the proposal for both 1823 and 1824.

1822 was to prove a mixed year, with two deaths and a birth in the family, and a signal honour being awarded to Nicolas. On 26 February Elisabeth's cousin Nicolas-Louis Benoist died aged 70 in Reims.[235] It had been at his house at *N° 27 rue de l'Arbalète* that Nicolas had been hiding in 1794 when he was arrested (see page 68). No doubt they had kept up a close family connection over the years.

Then on 19 July 1822, Nicolas's brother Jean-Baptiste died in Châlons–sur–Marne, also aged 70.[236] He had carried on the family tradition of running the Royal Palace Hotel until selling it in 1803. He had married Elisabeth's sister, Nicole-Sophie, in 1789. Nicole was still alive when her husband died; she died having been a widow for nearly thirteen years shortly before her 72nd birthday on 15 February 1835 in *l'hospice Saint-Maur* in Châlons.[237]

Of the original 11 children of Claude and Marie-Nicolle Appert, only Jules-Claude-Marie, now aged 76, and Nicolas, aged 72, were still alive.

About a month later, on Wednesday 21 August 1822, Nicolas and Elisabeth's granddaughter Céline Edmée was born to their daughter Amélie-Justine and her husband Jean-Louis Lefébure in *rue du Coq Saint Honoré* in Paris.[238] Céline is my wife's great-great grandmother.

It was also in 1822 that Nicolas may have been awarded the distinction of being named a *bienfaiteur de l'humanité*, a benefactor of mankind, by the *Société d'Encouragement pour l'Industrie Nationale*. There is some doubt as to whether this accolade was indeed awarded as records cannot be found to substantiate it. In later correspondence Nicolas never refers to it, even though he lists other prizes and distinctions. In my researches I have found many sources – although not contemporary ones – that claim this well-deserved title for Nicolas. However, there is a difference of opinion as to whether it was indeed the *Société d'Encouragement* or the English who granted him this title. I believe that, if anyone, it was the *Société*, because the title of *bienfaiteur de l'humanité* is one that appears again and again in 19th century French sources about various scientists – Louis Pasteur being perhaps the most prominent example. It seems a very French accolade therefore.

The earliest document I have found that states that the Society did honour him with the title is Kathleen Golden Bitting's tribute *"Un Bienfaiteur de l'Humanité* [a tribute to M. Nicolas Appert]" with text in English that was first published in 1924:

> Appert's genius in research coupled with the generous spirit caused the Society for the Encouragement of National Industry to bestow on him, in 1822, the title *"Un Bienfaiteur de l'Humanité,"* which he richly deserved, for he could have become wealthy by reserving his discoveries to his own advantage, as other countries as well as France undoubtedly would have paid well for a knowledge of the discoveries which he gave so freely. They have enabled countless millions to be made since, both in canning and in supplies and machinery, many of those profiting not even knowing the name nor giving a thought to the discoverer.[239]

Although Captain de Freycinet had returned from his

circumnavigation of the globe in late 1820, it was not until 1822 that he gave public support to Nicolas regarding the quality and usefulness of his preserved food. On 1 June 1822 he wrote an official report for the Navy Command in the form of a letter, contributed to the 1822 *Annales Maritimes et Coloniales*. Captain de Freycinet wrote:

Sir,

The preservation of food substances by the process of M. Appert is one of the most wonderful and most important discoveries that have been made for a long time to the benefit of navigators. Previously, the continual use of salted meat at sea accelerated the development of scurvy and one could not combat this unfortunate influence by having poultry and live cattle aboard, since they could only be kept alive with difficulty on the early days of the voyage.

Often on long voyages, one was reduced to desperate measures; the sick especially were deprived of the healthy food necessary for their recovery. Now Appert's preserves provide a perfect way to provision even the longest voyages: plants, meat, fish, and fresh dairy produce can be transported with confidence for an indefinite period, in all latitudes, under the most diverse temperatures, and everywhere the sailor can serve at his table healthy food, as pleasant as if he had been in port. In the circumnavigation that I have just completed, I had loaded aboard a large quantity of M. Appert's preserves; they perfectly passed, even beyond my expectations, all the tests to which I submitted them over the thirty-eight months of sailing.

Due recognition and fairness lead me to publicize these facts, so honourable for M. Appert; and I thought you would like to give them the publicity that they deserve, by printing my letter.

I have the honour of being etc.

L. DE FREYCINET,
Ship's Captain[240]

Just over a month later, Captain de Freycinet wrote a letter to The Society for the Encouragement of National Industry. The Society's Bulletin published the text, which concluded with:

> ...After these brief reflections on the advantages that must result from the wonderful discovery of M. Appert, I cannot help but have a painful feeling seeing this man, more than sixty years old, in a position approaching need.
>
> Limited in his resources, he cannot do all the good he conceives: his factory is languishing, while others seize the initiative and enrich themselves on the proceeds of his industry. The Society for Encouragement can give a new impetus to the useful establishment of M. Appert, pay the debt of recognition and acquire new titles to the gratitude of the friends of humanity and national prosperity.[241]

As a footnote, the Bulletin reminded its readers that M. Appert's factory was at *N° 17 rue Moreau*, while his goods could be bought at M. Labour's shop at *Hôtel des Américains*, *rue St. Honoré*, M. Leroy's at *N° 330 rue St. Honoré*, and M. Corcelet's *au Palais-Royal*.

According to the 1841 book *Les Artisans Illustres*, by Édouard Foucaud, the *Société d'Encouragement pour l'Industrie Nationale* awarded Nicolas 2,000 *francs* in 1822.[242] If so, it is likely that this was as a result of the intervention by the good Captain de Freycinet.

In his workshops in the *enclos des Mousquetaires* in the *rue Moreau*, Nicolas continued to experiment. He developed and improved an industrial sized autoclave, a type of pressure cooker. Just two years earlier, on 9 April 1820, Pierre Alexandre Lemare had taken out a patent for a "*marmite autoclave.*" The London "Literary Gazette and Journal of Belles Lettres, Arts, Sciences Etc for the year 1820" carried the following article:

Science and Gastronomy:- At a time when we see generals, physicians, and students, pretend to improve the difficult science of politics, we must not be surprised at seeing a skilful grammarian improve the art of cookery. M. Lemare, director of the Atheneum of Languages, has invented a utensil, which he calls *autoclave*. M. Lemare engages to dress his dinner in less than half an hour, and lately made the experiment with complete success before a numerous company. He had put into the vessel a piece of meat, vegetables and as much water as is necessary for a dish for five persons. The vessel was placed over a fire which was kept up with some pieces of charcoal. In 36 minutes the vessel was taken off, and left for a few minutes to cool; and the reporter affirms that the broth was excellent, and the meat thoroughly done. It is not necessary to open the pot to skim it, so much as once during the boiling, for at the end of the operation the scum is found at the bottom of the vessel and does not mix with the broth. The advantages of this *autoclavian* cookery are, 1$^{st.}$ that the soup is excellent, which is very natural, because the vessel is hermetically closed, and nothing is therefore lost; 2$^{d.}$ that produce is much increased by the quantity of jelly yielded by the bones; 3$^{d.}$ that the cookery is far more expeditious than in the ordinary kettles, &c. The mode of cookery will be highly advantageous to the poor, in particular.

We leave the detailed description of the *autoclave* to those journals that are especially devoted to such subjects. If satisfactory and repeated trials confirm the utility of the invention, it will become highly important in its results, as it will then be evident that cooking may be performed in much less than the usual time, and with one tenth part of the fuel now employed. M. Lemare's process is a very simple, and for that reason, very ingenious improvement of Papin's digester. It speaks much in favour of the invention that, as appears in a letter from the minister of the interior, the *autoclave* has been in use above a month in the school for the blind in Paris. Should it come into general use, M. Lemare will doubtless derive more profit from the sale of this apparatus than from all his discoveries in etymology and his excellent precepts on orthography; and this is in the nature of things. In this enlightened age, we undoubtedly set a high value on correctness of language but a well dressed dinner is far more valuable.[243]

In the same Journal, however, was also a brief description of an accident involving the new *autoclave* which was to have great repercussions:

Death of Naldi. – Poor Naldi, the admirable buffo of the King's Theatre, has met with a strange and untimely death at Paris. Going to dine with Garcia, it is stated in the journals, he stopped the valve of a new cooking apparatus, which burst and killed him on the spot. His companion was slightly hurt. A description of the *autoclave* (the machine which proved so fatal) will be found at page 506.[244]

The full story was carried a few days after it had happened in *Le Moniteur Universel* on the 17 December 1820:

Paris: 16 December

A horrible accident occurred at half past six in the evening, the day before yesterday, at the home of M. Garcia, which brought despair in the death of M. Naldi, artist of the *Théâtre Royal Italien*. This artist, invited to dinner by M. Garcia, had just arrived with his daughter and wife, and was examining the cooking pot which was being prepared in the fireplace by the accelerated process of *marmite autoclave*. The valve to release the pressure was operating normally and the operation was just about finished, when M. Naldi, by an imprudent and deadly mistake, stopped up, with the aid of the fireplace pincers, the conduit of the steam, and the heat built up by compression to such a point that the cover of the cooker, with a sudden explosion, struck M. Naldi on the forehead, opened his skull, and left him dead at the feet of his daughter. M. Garcia, standing behind his unfortunate friend, did not receive any serious wound; the steam only caused him a burn on the upper part of his face... The doctors, who came immediately, applied all their skills to M. Naldi; but all the effort was in vain; he was no more.

Guiseppe Naldi's funeral took place on Sunday 17 December in the church of Saint-Roch. He was buried in the Parisian cemetery of Père Lachaise. It was not until the end of the January following that the opera singer M. Garcia was well enough to resume his performances.

In Nicolas's fourth edition of his book, published eleven years later than this in 1831, he gave a very different view of events. In his version, Naldi was the owner of the autoclave and in trying to impress his guests he caused the fatal accident. Nicolas wrote:

Wholly appreciating the merit of the new discovery, Naldi was one of the first to obtain an autoclave. It served him for a long time with success. Enthusiastic, like all artists, he recommended his device everywhere, and provided everyone with the benefits of his knowledge. Some friends, to whom he had strongly recommended the autoclave's use, declared they would like to try it out. M. Naldi joyfully accepted this proposal, undertook to transport the pot to their house, and to make the stew himself.

They assembled on the agreed day: the meeting was large, all the guests were cheerful, and curious to see the experiment begin of which nobody foresaw the awful result.

M. Naldi announced that his stew would be cooked in 30 or 40 minutes; but he had not considered that the layout of the hearth had considerably delayed the operation. Instead of the type of stove he usually used, he was obliged to employ the heat of a chimney fire, which only heated the pot on one side, and which could not bring it quickly to the boil. This setback, which he had not foreseen, annoyed him greatly, and he tried in vain to overcome it by increasing the intensity of fire; and the poorly heated device resisted all his efforts.

Some jokes at his expense piqued him to the point of

forgetting all caution; and wanting absolutely to obtain the results that he had announced, he loaded the valve with all its weight to accelerate the boiling, and yet it still did not boil. By an inconceivable temerity he strongly pushed the top with a pair of pliers. The heat created by this additional load at the highest degree of expansion tore the device, with the lid lifting with a terrible explosion, smashing the head of the too careless Naldi.[245]

In spite of the rest of the world seeking to avoid the potential death threat from an autoclave, Nicolas saw an opportunity. He could branch out with his experiments using an autoclave, but the small domestic size would not be sufficient! He also would need to address the very real safety problems that the Lemare design had.

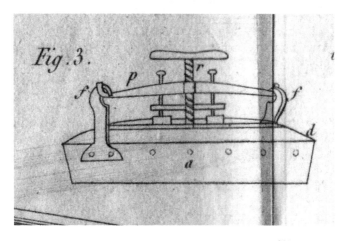

Appert's design for the lid of his autoclave[246]

(From the author's collection)

Nicolas firstly bought a 12 litre autoclave. After a few experiments he ordered, from the same workshop that created the Lemare autoclaves, another autoclave: this time its capacity would need to be 300 litres![247]

He adapted the design of the autoclave's lid and its fixings so that it could withstand a great deal more pressure. He included this design in his application for a patent for his method of extracting tallow in 1823.

Nicolas's improvements in the design of the autoclave enabled him to use capacities up to 400 litres.[248] Among his first uses for the autoclave was a new procedure for producing tallow for candles. Nicolas wrote in the Foreword of his 1831 edition of "The Book For All Households":

> In 1822, I was instructed by His Excellency the Minister of the Navy, to provide the food substances, treated according to my processes, to be stored aboard ships of the state and intended to supply patients. My wish was finally fulfilled: this happy circumstance for me was clear evidence that the goodness and effectiveness of my processes were finally recognized and they were now free from any criticism. I continued this service for several years and until the minister had established a factory in Bordeaux similar to mine.
>
> At that time, I often used up two or three cattle per day. It was then that I began my experiments on the melting of tallow using an autoclave. I managed to melt and clarify tallow and to pour it immediately into candles. There are details of these experiments in this fourth edition.[249]

In the early nineteenth century there were two main types of candle. The wealthier echelons of society used beeswax candles which burned without producing a smoky flame, giving off a sweet smell. Beeswax was also widely used in churches.

Most people, however, could not afford these beeswax candles, and instead used tallow candles. Tallow is rendered animal fat, usually of beef or mutton, but at a pinch any kitchen fats would do. Unfortunately there were many drawbacks with these cheaper candles. In the home, they burned with a foul smell and smoky flame.

At the slaughterhouses, the stench of the boilers used to obtain the animal fats was a significant public health hazard. Even worse than the smell was the fairly high likelihood of a fire spreading from the huge furnaces they used in their wooden buildings. Nicolas recalled such an incident:

> An accident occurred a few years ago, at the foundry in the slaughterhouse by the Fontainebleau Gate, and seriously attracted the authority's attention. The Count of Chabrol, Prefect of the Seine, assembled the master butchers of Paris: after having criticized a reprehensible carelessness, he bade them seek ways to operate in a way more consistent with public health and safety; the concern of this magistrate went so far as to designate a scientist, M. Darcet, as the person most capable by his understanding of being able to assist their research.
>
> The care thus taken was unproductive: what happened in this circumstance is what unfortunately happens almost always, the intentions of the Prefect were evaded, and the advice of M. Darcet was not followed, and things stayed as they were.[250]

For several hundred years, candle makers – or chandlers – had been organized into a guild in France, as they had been in England. As well as having their own shops, they often went from house to house making candles from the fats saved for that purpose from the kitchen. These guilds protected their own trade, as shown by a story that Nicolas went on to tell:

> At that time, I was busy preserving a large quantity of meat for the use of the Royal Navy. The butcher who provided me with oxen was a member of the guild of butchers; he told me of the intentions of the Prefect, which inspired me to use this

opportunity to try some experiments with my autoclave; here's how I operated.

I began by cutting ten pounds of tallow into very small pieces. After peeling them, I washed them several times, left them to soak for twenty-four hours and then drained them. Next I put them with three litres of water into a small autoclave with the capacity of twelve litres. I placed my device on the fire, after fixing the lid and putting on the valve, which I loaded gradually with the necessary weights to a pressure of one hundred and eighty degrees of heat.

After removing the heat and letting it cool, as usual, until the weight and the valve could be removed without producing steam, I then took the lid off the autoclave and I left it to cool, for a good hour. The tallow, which was perfectly melted, I removed from the top of the water, and I made it into a small cake. This first operation over, I poured the rest of the boiler water into a bowl to collect the little tallow contained therein.

When completely cool, I weighed the residues, and I calculated that the ten pounds of tallow had experienced a reduction of thirteen per cent, which when pressed, no longer had small membranes and was absolutely purged of fat and gelatinous juice. The experiment, carried out in the presence of my butcher, proved that the waste resulting from my melting was only half of that given by ordinary processes. He admitted also that my tallow was much purer, whiter and drier than from other foundries. Astonished by such results, he encouraged me to make further tests and to operate in larger quantities.

I was too pleased with my success to resist his appeals, and that evening I began a second experiment. This time, I made two hundred and sixty pounds of tallow in the autoclave, after having prepared it the way that I just mentioned above, and when it was taken from the fire and cooled, I found, uncovering the boiler, well melted and perfectly clear tallow. I removed it from above the water and placed it in containers. I placed the water which remained at the bottom of the autoclave in other vessels; after cooling, I separated the tallow which I then pressed, as in the first operation: the result produced a loss of twelve percent.

The beauty of this perfect tallow made me determined to try

immediately to make it into a candle. The master butcher, who had assiduously followed my operations, shared the methods with his foundry man, who was at the same time a chandler, and he recommended we send him the first samples from the mould.

The candles made from the tallow that Nicolas made were of a much higher quality than those that were usually available. Nicolas's workshop could melt the tallow, but he was not in a position to start to turn the tallow into candles. He thought to involve the chandler who had enthusiastically helped him with his first samples. However,

A new invention has not only to fight against the prejudices of the everyday routine; it also has to overcome resistance from special interests that it is likely to offend. The satisfactory results of my first two experiments decided me to take out a patent. I was convinced now that henceforth my method would be the only one adopted, and that no candle manufacturer would want to use other tallow than my melting.

While awaiting the moment to give my business this new extension which I thought possible, I continued to operate on my processes with full success. I managed to melt four times twelve hundred pounds of tallow branch.

I sent my first melting to the chandler who had taken my samples and had given them so much praise. I was not present to attend the handling, and soon I had time to repent of that, because, just days after the opening of the package he gave me, I recognized that he had deceived me, and that the candles did not come from my melting. I scolded him sharply, though he denied the fact; however, I paid for my tallow, and thus ends the first episode, but I was not finished, although I did not yet know how far the malice of a chandler could go!

In the meantime, a trader among my friends to whom I told my adventure, told me of another chandler, a "perfectly honest man," to whom, he assured me, I could speak with confidence. I hastened to send two hundred pounds of my tallow to him, and eight to ten days afterwards I received my candles. Would that I could have had such confidence that I could open this package and not consider it carefully, relying instead on the good faith of this "perfectly honest man!" However, after quite a long time, wishing to use these candles for my own use, I was greatly surprised to find them even worse than the other.

Such beginnings do nothing to encourage; anyway, I did not leave off while cursing, but continued to deliver my tallow to several other manufacturers of candles, all of whom served me with the same sensitivity!

I could hardly conceive how, after obtaining a perfectly good candle by my process, it could not be made into more than the common sort, for I was far from supposing that manufacturers were enough enemies of their own true interests to combine the pure tallow that I delivered to them with coarse tallow from the slaughterhouses. It was only with many new experiments that I achieved certainty of a fraud that thus affected my melting without improving theirs at all.

Disgusted by such dishonesty, I decided to make my candles myself, so my results returned to being absolutely similar to the first that I had achieved.

Not wanting to expose myself to more cheating, I stopped sending my tallow to be manufactured, and I postponed my operations until a more propitious time, and where I could manage all parts of the melting and the manufacture of candles.

A chain of circumstances since has always delayed this time, and now it is likely that I will not come back to this aim, but nevertheless, persuaded by my tests of the excellence of this process that I have just indicated, I thought it valuable to record it here, and even develop all the details concerning the melting of tallow by the autoclave.[251]

Nicolas filed for his patent for 5 years in due course on 24 April 1823. The patent stated:

Patent of Invention for five years:
For a new method to melt tallow in sealed apparatus,
To M. Appert, of Paris.

This method involves melting tallow in any enclosed container, of metal, glass, clay or sandstone: the pots known as *autoclaves* are very suitable for this purpose; heat is applied to the pots to a high temperature that depends on the quality of the raw material.

Method of operation:

An unpeeled stick of tallow is placed in the vessel with water; the proportions are one third water to two-thirds of tallow; the sealed vessel is then raised to a temperature of one hundred and fifteen to one hundred and thirty degrees, depending on the material; this level of heat is maintained for one hour, and then allowed to fall to about fifty degrees. The vessel is then opened, and the tallow is separated from the water using a pan, and placed in a cooling tub.

The tallow that results is dry and sound; as it is pure and not burned, the candle made from it is very white, does not run, lasts more than $\frac{1}{5}$ more than an ordinary candle, is not more expensive and has no odour when burned.

Among the advantages for public health and safety of this procedure is that it does not give off any odour or sickening or unhealthy smoke – not even in the room where it is made, whatever the size of vessel employed. This process cannot give rise to any danger of fire. [252]

Around this time Nicolas started to have difficulty with the government over the lease of *N° 17 rue Moreau*. In August 1817 there had been no doubt that the premises were to be rent free for Nicolas and his business. The government was already committed to paying the 4,000 *francs* until the end of the lease in June 1824, and was simply allowing Nicolas to have use of the premises. However, some change of heart had taken place among the ministers of Louis XVIII.

In early 1822 the prefect of Police had served notice on him that he was to be expelled from the premises. Nicolas wrote to the Minister of the Interior, His Excellency the Count of Corbière, and sent also several of his goods, either as an incentive to hear his plea or as an example of the benefit to society of the government's money![253] Unfortunately, neither the letter nor the preserved meat and vegetables did the trick. The Minister instructed the prefect of Police to remove him immediately from the premises – with the use of whatever sized armed force needed to overcome the workforce.

Either the Police were not keen to proceed or Nicolas was too difficult to remove: there was a stand-off for a while. This did not distract Nicolas from experimenting with the autoclave, achieving his patent for melting tallow, and developing his business further.

While expulsion from *Quinze-Vingts* was hanging over him, Nicolas began work on extracting gelatine from bones, bringing it to a successful conclusion by early 1824.

On Wednesday 3 March 1824 Antoine-Germain Labarraque read a report to the Society for the Encouragement of National Industry that he and two colleagues had prepared. The report covered Nicolas's preserving procedures, with which the Society were extremely familiar, and then his two new processes for melting tallow and for extracting gelatine.[254] In *Archives Des Découvertes et Des Inventions Nouvelles Pendant l'Année 1824,* there was a shortened version of the report:

GELATINE

A method for extracting gelatine from bones;
by M. Appert.

The bones forming the head of beef, and other fleshy parts of the head, are parboiled in cold water until the liquid becomes colourless and then they are boiled in water for a further time. This separates the carcase and the fleshy parts that are put aside to make meat juices... The bones are then placed in a pressure cooker, or autoclave, with a suitable amount of liquid, and are

Commemorative First Day Cover Postcard
5 March 1955

(From the author's collection)

heated in this device by fire. The gelatinous liquid leaving the autoclave is skimmed and then made to evaporate; the condensation is continued by means of steam, and then gelatine is cast in tablets, which are further dried. This gelatine has been found very good, and provided a broth comparable to the best meat broth.[255]

Shortly after this, the Society for the Encouragement of National Industry opened tins of preserved meat submitted by both Nicolas and his colleague from Nantes, once his retailer, M. Joseph Colin. Nicolas's tins were a huge 17 kg of various meats and poultry that had been placed aboard the corvette Lybia two years before.

On this occasion, the Society was convinced that the prize money should be awarded. Nicolas received the prize of 2,000 *francs* two weeks after the Society's decision at its meeting on Wednesday 10 November 1824.[256] News of the award was carried by publications in both France and England: in the *Revue Encyclopédique ou Analyse Raisonnée des Productions Les Plus Remarquables* of 1824 published in Paris[257], and in translation in the London Literary Gazette and Journal of Belles Lettres, Arts, Sciences, etc, for 1824. The English article said:

A premium of two thousand *francs*, for the preservation of alimentary substances, by a process executed on a larger scale than that proposed by M. Appert, (such were the terms of the notice) to M. Appert himself, he having given a fuller development to his method. By order of his Excellency the Minister of the Navy, two vases, each, containing sixty pounds of beef, and of gelatine prepared by M. Appert, were embarked for the island of Bourbon in the year 1822, and have returned to France in the highest state of preservation. It is true, that one of these vases having been opened while the vessel was under the equator, the substances it contained experienced some alteration; but it has been positively ascertained that this accident proceeded merely from a defect in the soldering of the vase. This experiment (says the reporter) proves the possibility of furnishing our ships with fresh provisions, whatever may be the length of the voyage; and foreigners will no longer be able to boast that they alone enjoy the benefits of a discovery which belongs to France, and which is of important consequence to humanity in general.[258]

The island of Bourbon is now known as Réunion, to the east of Madagascar in the Indian Ocean.

Nicolas received a further accolade in 1824. He had attended meetings of the Society for the Encouragement of National Industry for a long time, and had made contributions to the meetings on many occasions. Finally, the Society admitted him as a member.

LISTE des membres de la Société admis pendant l'année 1824.

APPERT, chimiste, auteur du procédé pour préparer les substances alimentaires, rue Moreau, n°. 17, faubourg Saint-Antoine.

Nicolas Appert finally admitted to
La Société d'Encouragement pour l'Industrie Nationale
in 1824[259]

Just prior to these events, on 22 September 1824, Nicolas received a further ultimatum about his premises at the *Quinze-Vingts*. It was by this time beyond the original tenure of the government, which had expired in June 1824. The ultimatum stated that he must either leave the premises immediately or pay the huge sum of 8,320 *francs* in rent. With so much invested in the business Nicolas had little choice but to start paying rent and so he took out a three year lease, starting from 1 January 1825.[260] Nicolas did not, however, bow to this quietly. He wrote again to the Minister of the Interior in mid-February 1825 explaining again the circumstances of the original gift of the premises and detailing everything that he had been able to achieve as a result. He concluded with an appeal:

> I thought, having arrived at 75 years of age of a life completely devoted to science and humanity, to have nothing more than to die in peace with my family and friends, when you thought, my Lord, of having to remove me from the premises that I held of the magnificence of the government; premises that I considered as usufruct as a reward, an incentive… I come, my Lord, to implore you to grant me relief or a financial gift… I have sacrificed everything for humanity throughout my entire life.[261]

In spite of these and other entreaties, including by the Society for the Encouragement of National Industry and by the Bureau of Arts and Manufacturing, Nicolas did not get either a reduction in his rent or an allowance to help him pay.

There was at this time a new monarch and government in France. Louis XVIII had died on 16 September 1824 and, in the only peaceful succession of any sort in 19th century France, his brother the *comte d'Artois* became King Charles X. Charles was crowned at Reims Cathedral, the ancient traditional venue for coronations of Kings of France, on Saturday 28 May 1825.

Just four weeks prior to this, on Saturday 30 April 1825, Nicolas's last surviving brother, Jules-Claude-Marie died aged 79.[262] Jules-Claude-Marie had continued to live in Châlons–sur–Marne, as it was by this time called, and had been a *marchand épicier*, or grocer, in the *rue Saint Jacques*, the same road as the Royal Palace Hotel (now the *rue Léon Bourgeois*). His death was registered by his son Jean Baptiste Nicolas Appert. On the death certificate Jules-Claude-Marie was called a widower, and so his wife, Jeanne Catherine, had already died by this date. The occasion when Nicolas, employed as a catering cadet in Zweibrücken, had been allowed to travel back to Châlons to attend Jules and Jeanne's wedding in 1773 must have seemed a very dim memory.

In 1826 (and reprinted in 1827), Nicolas published his method for extracting gelatine that he had presented to *la Société d'Encouragement pour l'Industrie Nationale* two years previously. The publication was called *Notice sur la dépuration de la gélatine des os et rendue propre à la clarification des vins, eaux de vie, liqueurs, etc.*, published by Éverat of Paris. He wrote this 48 page pamphlet in response to a harsh and forceful attack that had been published by M. P. Gratien Lainé. His wife was, like Nicolas, engaged in experiments to produce gelatine. She contributed, as did Nicolas, to the 1827 *Exposition* (see below) where she received an "honourable mention."

I have found three publications by M. Lainé, a hardware merchant store owner, all described in *La France Littéraire, ou Dictionnaire Bibliographique* by J-M. Quérard, Volume 4, 1830.[263]

The first publication is addressed to "Messrs the President and Members of the Chambers of Deputies," a 24 page booklet published in 1825 by Leblanc in Paris. However, I do not know the content of the booklet.

The second is a letter to a M. Jacqueminot de Pampleune, again published in 1825 by Leblanc of Paris. This is a more substantial piece of work, running to 112 pages.

Either of these two could be the offending article. What is certain is that Nicolas felt that he needed to set the record straight in terms of how he made his gelatine, its quality and its purity. He clearly felt stung by the injustice of whatever M. Lainé had written.

The third of M. Lainé's publications was printed by Moessard of Paris in 1828 and was entitled as follows:

> To M. Appert,
> Inventor of slander, maker of poor stewed meat only fit to be thrown away, and of gelatine that spoils wine.

No love lost there, then! Apart from the information that it contains 36 pages, sadly I do not know the contents of this publication either. However, this third publication by M. Lainé must have been in response to Nicolas's *Notice sur la dépuration de la gélatine* published in 1826.

This seems to have been the end of the acrimony between these two men. Just three years after that last publication, Nicolas's fourth edition of "The Book For All Households" makes no mention at all of the feud. Indeed, they became near neighbours in *rue de Paradis* in 1828, when Nicolas moved to *N° 16*, with *M. et Mme Lainé* residing at *N° 10*.[264]

Nicolas had unsuccessfully exhibited his preserved food at the fourth *L'Exposition de l'Industrie Française* in 1806 at the height of Napoleon's power. International events prevented the Exposition being held again until 1819. Nicolas took no part in that Exposition, or in the one following in 1823.

On Wednesday 1 August 1827 the Seventh National Exposition of the Products of French Industry opened in the Courtyard of the Louvre, lasting 60 days and boasting 1695 exhibitors. Gold Medal winners had to be content with the glory of victory without the invitation to a meal with Napoleon, as had happened at the 1802 Exposition, as he had died six years earlier on 5 May 1821 in exile over 4,000 miles away at Longwood on St. Helena.

In spite of the poor state of the country's finances under

an increasingly unpopular King Charles X, a record number of exhibitors set up their stands. In 1828 the *Exposition de 1827: Rapport du Jury Central sur les Produits de l'Industrie Française* published a complete description of all the prize winners. There were 42 categories in the exhibition, which were split down into 184 sections that were to be judged individually. Overall, for the 1,695 exhibitors, there were 1,254 prizes awarded, of which only 104 were Gold Medals. Not every section winner merited the coveted *médaille d'or*.

Nicolas exhibited in the *Economie Domestique* category, under Section IV *Substances Alimentaires*, Article 1 *Conservation des Comestibles*. He was successful in winning the Gold Medal for his products. This success was recorded on page 412 of the *Rapport du Jury Central sur les Produits de l'Industrie Française* with the following citation:

Gold Medal

M. APPERT of 7 (sic) *rue Moreau*, Paris

The brief was to prepare a complete assortment of types of food, together with several products prepared with gelatine extracted from bones, composed of healthy yet inexpensive items.

Everyone knows the success achieved by M. Appert in the art of preserving food, and the positive impact this has had on the health of sailors. His processes are remarkable in that they are of general application, and that while offering to the rich new pleasures, they bring well-being into the least of households.

A gold medal is awarded to M. Appert.

Section IV.

Substances alimentaires.

———

Article premier.

Conservation des Comestibles.

Médaille M. Appert, à Paris, rue Moreau, n.° 7,
d'or.

A exposé un assortiment complet de substances alimentaires, ainsi que différens produits qu'il prépare avec la gélatine extraite des os, et qui sont susceptibles de former une nourriture à-la-fois saine et peu coûteuse.

Tout le monde connaît les succès obtenus par M. *Appert* dans l'art de conserver les comestibles, et l'influence favorable qu'ils ont eue sur la santé des marins. Ses procédés ont cela de remarquable qu'ils sont d'une application générale, et qu'en offrant au riche des jouissances nouvelles, ils portent le bien-être dans l'intérieur des moindres ménages.

Une médaille d'or est décernée à M. *Appert.*

The report of Nicolas's Gold Medal
in the 1827 *Exposition*[265]

The next Parisian Exposition was in 1834, under Louis Philippe I King of the French, four years after Charles X had been forced to abdicate. In spite of his success in 1827, Nicolas did not participate in 1834. Perhaps, having achieved the Gold Medal, he felt that he had attained the recognition he wanted.

In his factory, Nicolas was busily making more progress. He used his large autoclaves to create another new invention, a bouillon tablet, and to perfect the procedure for extracting gelatine from bones without using acid.

Nicolas was supplied with more than 3,000 ducks per month and with beef delivered direct, fresh from the slaughterhouse.[266] To create the bouillon tablets, the forerunner of today's stock cubes, he proceeded in a similar fashion to that described above for the extraction of gelatine. The meat was cooked in the autoclave several times, with water being replaced each time so that the fat would be reduced. This would continue until the flesh fell away from the bones. Nicolas would then use the meat either to create more tinned broth or by pressing and dehydrating it to produce the bouillon tablets.

For the bouillon tablets, the broth was then spread out over a large surface to allow for evaporation, all the while being gently heated, while the broth flowed continuously – see the Plate below.

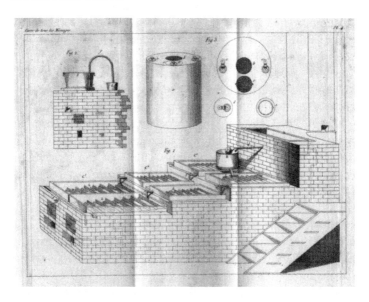

The Evaporator Apparatus for the Bouillon tablets
(From the author's collection)[267]

The whole procedure took in excess of three days. The resulting material was then poured and pressed into moulded sheets 12 inches by 8 inches by 1 inch deep. They were then left to cool.

Having been left like this for two more days, the bouillon then spent a third day in an oven being gently heated to 18 degrees on the Réaumur scale (22.5° C) in order to desiccate it fully. Each tray was then cut into 10 tablets. Nicolas concludes his description with:

> Speed and cleanliness are the two prerequisites in the operations that I have just described; one is of benefit to the manufacturer and the other to consumer health.[268]

Throughout his 1831 book, Nicolas quotes temperatures, as above, in the Réaumur scale. René Antoine Ferchault de Réaumur (1683 – 1747) was a French scientist who, among other things, was a mathematician, a physicist, an entomologist and an early student of animal behaviour. In 1731 he proposed a temperature scale based on an 80° difference between the freezing and boiling points of water – another example of the *système vicésimal*, based on the number 20. The Réaumur scale gained widespread popularity especially in France, Germany and Russia throughout the eighteenth century and into the nineteenth. However, in France it was officially replaced by the Celsius scale in the 1790s – one of the many measurements that went decimal during the Revolution.

The Réaumur scale evidently still lives on today, being used in measuring the milk temperature in cheese, especially in Switzerland and Italy. It is interesting that Nicolas was still using this scale in France as late as the 1830s; he also gave lengths in feet and inches and weights in pounds, although he used litres for capacity. Perhaps his bad experience during the Revolution had led him to be something of a reactionary!

Nicolas's last invention was the production, again by virtue of his autoclaves, of calf's-foot jelly. This sweet gelatine was very popular as a dessert. In the 1834 fourth edition of "The Book For All Households" Nicolas describes how to go about the *Extraction de l'huile de pied de bœuf* by a similar approach to extracting gelatine from bones.[269]

On Monday 31 December 1827, at the end of his three-year lease, Nicolas ceased renting the expensive premises at *Quinze-Vingts*. After just over ten years there he moved, aged 78, to what proved to be his last address in Paris, at *N°16 rue du Paradis* in the Marais district. This move was a distance of about a mile back towards where he had first lived in Paris before the 1789 Revolution in the *rue des Lombards*.

Nicolas Appert: a sculpture by Roger Marion (1934 –)

Erected 2010 in Malataverne, France,
by Lagarde Autoclaves, of
N° 258 impasse Nicolas Appert, Malataverne[270]

Chapter 11

Rue du Paradis, Paris: 1828 – 1836

The first chapter of Nicolas's fourth edition of his "Book For All Households," published in 1831, is devoted to a thorough description of the *atelier Appert* at *N° 16 rue du Paradis*, and the various utensils and equipment used in his many processes. No doubt it took some time after moving in on 1 January 1828 to reach the fully working Appert business he describes.

Nicolas wrote:

Description of the workshops and apparatus that I have established for the complete operation of my process:

The first room on the ground floor, 55 feet in length by 28 feet wide, is divided over its length into six parts:

The first is for the shipments, packaging and so on. The second forms the store for those preparations that are manufactured and intended for sale. The third one, more spacious than its predecessors, is where the butcher's meat, poultry and game are prepared and made ready for cooking.

The fourth, north-facing, contains the pantry and office, separated from each other by a partition. The fifth one, to the side and also facing north, is fitted around its edges with rods or supports to which can be hooked up at once three or four oxen.

In this room are placed various objects used in the process of sealing bottles, etc, namely:

1st   A reel for the wire used to tie up the bottles etc.
2nd   A small turning machine to twist the wire.

3rd Two jaws to lever and compress small and large caps.

4th A stool mounted on five legs, to use while fastening wire.

5th A "bottle-boot" - a block mounted on three feet, topped with a strong bat to use in sealing.

6th Pointed pincers and shears to cut the wire on the cap. With this new invention one is able to wring advantage from the wire and cut it, without being obliged to use the tongs and turn the shears.

7th Shears, used to cut the wire into two equal parts, while on the reel.

8th A combined hook and corkscrew; the hook is designed to cut under the ring of wire that ties the bottles and jars. The corkscrew is used for large corks.

9th A sufficient quantity of bags used to wrap bottles and other vessels.

10th Two leather-covered stools, padded with hay, which are used when compressing the objects to be enclosed in vessels.

11th A press for the juices of plants, fruits, herbs and grapes, with terrines, vessels, sieves, and all that is necessary.

The sixth and last part is the kitchen. It is furnished with all its utensils, and seven stoves for the preparation of sauces, stir-fries, etc; a bench for grills; and a turn-spit to roast up to 50 or 60 pounds of beef.

In the Hall, by the way out, is a large beam furnished with weights.

Beyond the Hall is the tinsmith's workshop where the tins are made; it is divided into two parts each about 15 feet in length and 28 feet wide. Twenty-five to thirty workers can work there easily.

Further on, on the same floor, and turning to the right, is a very large room 150 feet long by 28 feet wide and 17 high, divided into six parts.

The first two, as you enter from the courtyard, are 60 feet long overall. These form the laboratory where food is cooked by the application of heat and the water-bath, or by steam, in order to clarify or reduce. In these two rooms thirteen brick furnaces, each 4 feet high by 4 feet wide, have been built.[271]

The description continues, itemising each cooker and furnace, varied sizes of autoclave, and the tin moulds used to cool gelatine tablets. The impression is of a very large factory, with its processes well designed to move from room to room, with the need for a large workforce to operate everything.

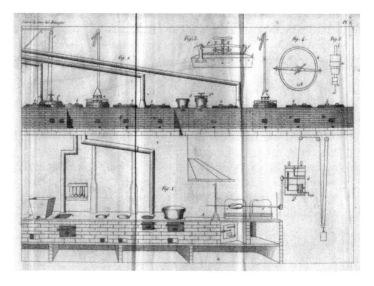

Some of the 13 stoves described opposite.

Nicolas's workshop at *N° 16 rue du Paradis*

(From the author's collection)[272]

Perhaps the biggest improvement that Nicolas made at this time was to create his own tinsmithy on site at *N° 16 rue du Paradis*. This enabled him to keep a close eye on the quality of the tin cans produced, and also to cut production costs as far as possible. He wrote about the problems he faced with French tin:

> The perfect preservation of food substances depends to a large extent on the perfection of the metal employed in the manufacture of the cans. It is important to record here a few remarks concerning the quality of tin that we make in France.
>
> The prodigious quantity that I have used for the manufacture of more than a hundred thousand tins of all sizes, has enabled me to be in a position to make a number of observations, from experience and all too often at my expense, regarding its imperfections.
>
> Of all our factories, those of *Chaudeau* and of *Bains* are the two which provide the quality of tin that is the most appropriate to my use; nevertheless, in spite of their superiority above all the others, they are far from having attained perfection, and their products leave still much to be desired, especially because of the continual differences in their quality which ought to be uniformly the same. These faults in manufacture have caused me huge losses, and have necessitated my sending back considerable quantities to these two establishments...[273]

It is surprising that Nicolas did not create his own tinsmithy until 1828, since he would have wanted to do so since his return from England in 1814. Describing his approach, Nicolas wrote:

> In adopting the use of tin cans, the first necessity is to attach a good tinsmith to my factory, whom I trained myself, and whom I can oversee. When, by dint of time and patience, I had brought this to the point I desired, I put my foreman in charge and entrusted him with about 15 workmen, whom he instructed in turn, at my expense.
>
> I relied entirely on him to distribute the work to each one, reserving to myself only to watch to check that only the more intelligent workers were put to the more difficult work, in appearance a simple thing yet foremen do not always think of it due either to carelessness or to other less blameworthy reasons.

Here are the details of the various operations required to give the perfect conditions for my cans: depending on the nature of the preserves that I propose to make, I calculate the approximate number I need of a particular size; my foreman first busies himself with cutting out the cans, which he then distributes to the workmen responsible for shaping them. Then another workman welds both ends, which must overlap by 4 or 5 *lignes* in order to increase the structural solidity and give the correct shape of coupling.

The first weld must be of a generous depth and made with all possible precision. It must then be covered on the inside with the same accuracy. The sides thus arranged the foreman cuts the bases, whose diameter exceeds the perimeter of the sides by 2 to 3 *lignes*; this surplus must again be folded with precision in order to fit the sides to the base.

After having adjusted the base, the inside is soldered to the exterior, so that the weld can seal the container to make one body... Next, the inside of the base and perimeter is lined with a little tin, taking care not to damage the outer lining, which would certainly happen if the metal were too hot.

The lids are cut to the same diameter as the bases; they are also folded back onto the sides. When they are finished, they are closed with a cutter of diameter of 6 *lignes*. They can then be pierced on the side a good inch from the edge.[274]

Nicolas employed up to thirty workmen in the smithy, producing up to 1,500 tins per month.

Tins of preserved food, whether from Appert or Donkin & Hall, his English competitor, started to be found around the world. In fact, this was true from before his time at the *rue du Paradis*. In the 1841 edition of Foucaud's *Les Artisans Illustres* while discussing the merits of Appert's discovery, the story is told of the luck of Captain Ross:

Captain Sir John Ross, in his account of his voyage to the arctic regions in 1833, mentions having found, upon the banks of Prince Regent's Strait, cans of Donkin's food preserved according to Appert's method. These had been left there in

1825, by Captain Parry, after the shipwreck of his vessel, the Fury; and, although exposed to the injuries of the weather during a space of four years, every article was as fresh as on the day they underwent the operation. By this fortunate encounter, Ross's vessel was replenished.[275]

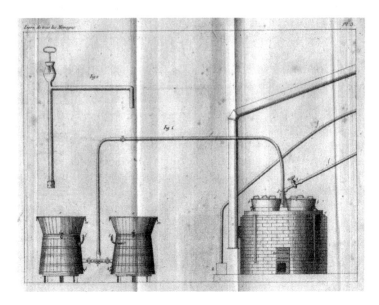

Nicolas's workshop at *N° 16 rue du Paradis*

(From the author's collection)[276]

One of the tins from the 1825 expedition was on show at the 1851 Great Exhibition in London. According to Chambers Edinburgh Journal of Saturday 23 October 1852:

But among the contributions … may be mentioned those of Mr Gamble, which comprised, among others, a canister of preserved boiled mutton, which had been prepared for the arctic expedition in 1824; many such canisters were landed at

Fury Beach in Prince Regent's Inlet; they were found by Sir John Ross at that spot in 1833 in a perfect state, and again by Sir James Ross in 1849, the meat being as sweet and wholesome as when prepared a quarter of a century before.[277]

These reports tell only a little part of this thrilling tale of arctic exploration. Captain William Parry had been trying to find the North-West Passage with two ships, the Fury and the Hecla. The two ships were held up over the arctic winter in Prince Regent's Inlet, from September 1824 to July 1825. Then the Fury suffered irreparable damage from the ice pushing it onto the shore and the crew had to join the Hecla. Parry then abandoned the attempt to find the North-West Passage and made safely for England.

This experience pales into insignificance when compared with Captain John Ross and the crew of the Victory. Setting out in 1829, they sailed beyond the point Parry had reached in 1825. Their ship then got caught in the ice and they had to spend the next four years in the arctic! No explorer before had spent anything like that amount of time there and survived. In all they lost only three crew members. They explored on foot the regions around, with the help of some Inuit who settled nearby, and John Ross's nephew, James Ross, located the magnetic north pole. By 1832, the captain and crew decided to abandon the Victory and walked to the shipwrecked Fury, where they ate canned food and built a shelter. Having repaired the Fury's longboats, they rowed to safety through a break in the ice in August 1833, and were picked up by a whaling ship.

For Nicolas, 1828 was both a very busy year, settling into new premises in the *rue du Paradis,* and another year of deaths in the family. His daughter Amélie-Justine and her husband Jean-Louis only had thirteen years of marriage together. When their daughter Céline Edmée was 5 years old, on Thursday 20 March 1828, Jean-Louis died. He was just 34 years old.

He died in Pointe-à-Pitre, in Guadeloupe, which had been a French colony since 1764. I do not know how long prior to this he had taken the post of *huissier*, or court bailiff, at Pointe-à-Pitre. Subsequently he became *commis à la poste*, post officer, there. I assume that his family went with him and then sadly made their way back to Paris after his death.[278]

Then on Sunday 29 June 1828, Nicolas's second daughter Aglaë-Françoise died aged 39. Her daughter Athenaïs Louisa Joséphine was just four days off her 10th birthday. Athenaïs was then looked after by Joseph Marie Barbieri, according to the terms of her mother's will. Athenaïs went on to marry Emile Hamelin on Thursday 7 February 1839 in Paris, giving birth to their first daughter Camille Sophie Joséphine a year and a day later. It is unlikely that Nicolas knew either his granddaughter or his great granddaughter due to the family estrangement.

In fact, the Appert family had probably fragmented even further by this date – Nicolas and Elisabeth must have parted. In the last will and testament of their estranged daughter, Aglaë-Françoise, it gives Nicolas's address as *Quinze-Vingts*, but Elisabeth's as *N° 8 rue Duras*, Paris, about 4 miles to the north west.[279]

The last date I can certainly link Nicolas and Elisabeth together was at Massy, where they were both witnesses to the wedding of their daughter Amélie-Justine to Jean-Louis Lefébure in April 1815. Their enforced move to Paris followed soon after to the *rue Cassette*, and then in 1817 to *Quinze-Vingts*. Nicolas moved from *Quinze-Vingts* at the end of 1827, and so the estrangement must have taken place at some time between 1817 and that date. Perhaps Nicolas's single-mindedness in pursuing his researches finally split the marriage. It is quite possible to imagine by the 1820s, with Nicolas in his seventies and Elisabeth in her sixties, that

Elisabeth did not want to face starting all over again building a business. Perhaps she spent too many lonely evenings while Nicolas was busy with his autoclaves and boilers.

Commemorative stamp issued 1 July 2010
by the Principality of Monaco
for the bicentenary of the publication of Nicolas Appert's book.
Designed by Créaphil and engraved by Pierre Albuisson (1952-)

(From the author's collection)

It is possible that Aglaë-Françoise becoming an unmarried mother in 1818 had been the difficulty that had divided them, perhaps with Elisabeth joining her daughter. However, a very poignant phrase in Aglaë-Françoise's will said that she left her 10 year old daughter to Joseph Barbieri "her only friend." I think that if her mother had remained as a support she would probably have been mentioned there too.

On Tuesday 17 November 1829 Nicolas celebrated his 80th birthday. I wonder if he had any family around him to mark the occasion. None of his brothers were still alive; one of his five children had also died. We can only hope that he was on good terms still with his remaining children: Charles-Pierre-Nicolas would be aged 43 and no doubt installed as *professeur* in Paris by now. Elisabeth Marie Nicole, the oldest daughter, would be 42, and married to a M. Ravenel. Amélie-Justine, aged 36, and her daughter Céline Edmée aged 7, would be grieving the loss of husband and father Jean-Louis. They might not yet even have returned from Pointe-à-Pitre. His youngest daughter, Angélique Eloïse, about whom I know no more than details of her birth and baptism, would be aged 34.

On Wednesday 24 February 1830 Nicolas attended the Society for the Encouragement of National Industry and made another of his many contributions to the meeting. He described the problems associated with producing cans made of tin, illustrating the difficulties from his vast experience. He then proposed that the Society should commission research, by the usual means of a prize, into using wrought iron or other material that might prove more consistently successful.[280]

At the 7 April meeting the Society indeed proposed a prize, to be awarded in 1832, of 2,000 *francs* to the person who could produce containers in wrought iron or other metal of similar strength, constructed in such a way that the containers could be reused.[281] This prize was never won in spite of its reissue over the next few years until 1838.

Meanwhile, Nicolas was about to live through his second experience of Revolution in Paris. As in 1789, there was an economic background to the troubles. Bread prices were going higher and higher; wages were being cut; nearly 65,000 Parisians were unemployed and becoming more desperate by the day.

The government of Charles X, which had tried to strike the balance of a constitutional monarchy, had run into great difficulties. Charles and the Chamber of Deputies were in dispute over the king's prerogative to appoint his own ministers. In this degenerating situation, Charles tried to assume emergency powers under Article 14 of the Charter that had been the basis of the Restoration of the monarchy under Louis XVIII.

Charles proclaimed the four July Ordinances, which were printed in the *Moniteur* newspaper on Monday 26 July 1830, an uncomfortably hot day. The first imposed censorship on the press; the second dissolved the Chamber of Deputies; the third, by far the most reaching, reduced the electorate by about three-quarters, making it far more aristocratic, and set rules for the elections to a new Chamber of Deputies; the fourth gave the dates for the next elections, to be held in September 1830.

There was instant uproar in Paris. The "Three Glorious Days" followed – Tuesday 27 to Thursday 29 July – which saw scenes reminiscent of the July forty-one years before with barricades and street battles between the people and the army who were trying to restore order. By the next day, the Bourbon dynasty was effectively over.

On 2 August, Charles abdicated and soon after left for exile, initially to England. The Lieutenant-Generalcy of the kingdom was given to the younger branch of the royal family in the person of Louis Philippe *duc d'Orléans*. Charles had abdicated in favour of his 10 year old grandson, whom he hailed as Henri V. However, the Chamber of Deputies invited Louis Philippe to become King of the French on 9 August 1830. Thus was installed what became known as the July Monarchy, with Louis Philippe reigning until a third revolution in 1848 deposed him in favour of the Second Republic. Louis Philippe was France's last king.

Nicolas played no part in this second revolution in 1830. No doubt his age had something to do with it, but he was also probably too busy re-writing his Book For All Households. On the title page, Nicolas described himself as "Former Confectioner and Distiller, Catering Student of the ducal house of Christian IV, a member of the Society for the Encouragement of National Industry." This 4th Edition was much larger than the previous (1813) edition, containing new procedures, experiments and observations. The book was published (as had the 3rd edition been) by Barrois the Elder, at *Nº 15 rue des Beaux-Arts*, in Paris in 1831, selling for 5 *francs*.

The Book begins with both a rationale for the new edition and an indication of the breadth of its contents. In its "Announcement of the Fourth Edition" on the first pages, Nicolas wrote:

> For over twenty years, since the first edition of the "Book For All Households" appeared, constant and multiplied successes have shown both the goodness and the effectiveness of my method. Many agree and consider my process as the best that can be used, and yet one can only find in the various published books an unclear, incomplete and inaccurate analysis of the means of preservation that I have made known.
>
> Learned societies have not stopped, during the same space of time, addressing the preservation of food substances. They proposed prizes to draw attention to this important subject. I say this with pride and with great satisfaction: there has not been published any process which was superior to mine or that presented as much guarantee of perfect success.

All these considerations have led me to publish a new edition of the "Book For All Households." I have reviewed it with great care, and I wanted to make it as worthy of the welcome that the public has given to previous editions. It contains the faithful exposition of all my works and the results of my long experience. I have catalogued them without reservation or hesitation.

After the destruction of my factory in Massy, as a result of the invasions of 1814 and 1815, I was forced to flee to Paris. I managed to save a few appliances, and I continued to involve myself in my operations. The Government having then granted me vast and convenient premises in the *Quinze-Vingts*, it was there that, by new research and experiments confirmed by persistent practice, I was able to simplify my processes, to introduce more economy, and to discover the improvements that I now publish in this fourth edition.

I have obtained most satisfying results from the autoclave. As soon as people overcome the fears that the machine inspires, and become familiar with its use, I have no doubt that the autoclave will be more generally used.

More can be found in this edition than in previous ones:

> Everything that relates to the manufacture of cans of tin and iron, for the preservation of food substances;
> The way to prepare and arrange the animal substances to be preserved by these processes;
> A new way to preserve wines whose delicacy will not allow either transport by sea or storage in many cellars;
> All my work with the autoclave or pressure cooker, with instruction on how to manage it;
> A new process for the extraction of bone gelatine, without using acid;
> The production of economical bouillon tablets;
> The extraction of calf's foot jelly, so useful in the arts;
> The melting and clarification of tallow and how to make it into candles.[282]

Occasionally, Nicolas gets carried away in the book, as here from the preface:

> It is for you particularly that he writes, tender and interested mothers, who are for your families a second providence. Hasten to put these processes into practice; hasten to collect carefully superfluous fruits, vegetables such as the favourable seasons offer in abundance, and whose maturity will all too soon deprive you of them. A day will come when, in the grim winter, the burning mouth of your sick children will be deliciously refreshed by these beneficial substances. A day will come when you offer, with a sweet satisfaction, these pleasant vegetables and delicate fruits that your foresight will have kept. The pleasure will be the recognition, the happiness of your family will be your reward, and, to do so much good, you simply have to wish to do it.[283]

However, on the whole the book is a treasure trove of practical detail. The chapter headings convey the breadth of the book:

1. Description of the workshops and apparatus that I have established for the complete operation of my process
2. Bottles and glass jars – corks – wiring up the bottles – stone jars
3. Cans of tin and wrought iron
4. Of the Water-bath
5. Description of the processes which constitute my method; its particular and specific application to each type of food to be preserved
6. Preparation of the substances destined to be preserved in cans
7. How to make use of the substances prepared and stored
8. Of autoclaves and the manner of their operation
9. Extraction of gelatine from bones, by the method of boiler compression or autoclave, without using muriatic acid
10. Extraction of calf's foot jelly
11. Melting tallow

Nicolas then appended a section of *pièces justificatives*, as in previous editions but much enlarged, that had given great support over the preceding thirty years to his methods.

As far as I can discover, this Fourth Edition has only been translated into English once, by Kathleen Golden Bitting, published in the USA in 1921.

On 19 October 1831, Denis-Placide Bouriat congratulated Nicolas on the new edition of his book at a meeting of the Society for the Encouragement of National Industry at their headquarters at the Boulogne Hotel, *N° 42 rue de Bacq*:

Report by M. Bouriat, on behalf of the Committee of the Economic Arts, on a work entitled *Le livre de tous les ménages ou l'Art de conserver pendant plusieurs années toutes les substances animales et végétales,* by M. Appert.

Gentlemen, a copy in octavo of the 4th edition of "The Art of Preserving Food Substances" was sent to you by M. Appert, as a humble tribute to the continued interest you have taken in the work which he has undertaken for over twenty years. Your Committee on Economic Arts was charged with the task of reviewing this book, and saw with pleasure that M. Appert had enlarged this fourth edition with various methods which did not exist in earlier editions, and many of them, though strangers to the culinary arts, are the result of many experiments, which, according to the author, have been successful: these are, for example, melting tallow branch, the extraction of calf's foot jelly, a description of his workshops and vast laboratories, with illustrations; how to keep wines at sea or in stores, etc. etc. . It also describes new processes to preserve a large volume of truffles, peas, asparagus, cauliflower and many other substances, and methods of extracting gelatin from various parts of animals. He also cites defects that sometimes occur in sheets of tin, and how to recognize if the cans made of this metal are likely to preserve the substances enclosed.

LE LIVRE

DE TOUS LES MÉNAGES,

ou

L'ART DE CONSERVER,

PENDANT PLUSIEURS ANNÉES,

TOUTES LES SUBSTANCES ANIMALES
ET VÉGÉTALES;

PAR M. APPERT,

Ancien Confiseur et Distillateur, Élève de la bouche de la maison ducale
de Christian IV, membre de la Société d'Encouragement pour l'industrie
nationale.

QUATRIÈME ÉDITION,

REVUE ET AUGMENTÉE DE PROCÉDÉS NOUVEAUX, D'EXPÉRIENCES
ET D'OBSERVATIONS NOUVELLES.

« J'ai pensé que votre découverte méritait un témoignage
« particulier de la bienveillance du gouvernement. »
Lettre de S. Exc. le MINISTRE DE L'INTÉRIEUR.

A PARIS,

CHEZ BARROIS L'AINÉ, LIBRAIRE,
RUE DES BEAUX-ARTS, N° 15;
L'AUTEUR, RUE DU PARADIS, N° 16, AU MARAIS.

1831.

Title page of Nicolas's Fourth Edition

(From the author's collection)

Your Committee thinks that we should be grateful to M. Appert for the constant zeal that he brings in order to create general-purpose methods for the preservation of food substances, all of which cost him pains, money and care. We see with satisfaction that this zeal has not been fruitless, since already many families use it to fulfil their needs, and that good housekeepers in all classes of society concern themselves, whether in the town or in the countryside, in the preparation, or in supervising the preparation, of the objects they wish to preserve, according to the methods specified by the author, and thus enjoy throughout the year products that nature offers only in a single season.

This fourth edition demonstrates that the first three are sold out and are therefore in the hands of many people who repeat the processes of the author for their use. They can engage in this kind of domestic economy with even greater ease now with the operations herein clearly detailed and with all restrictions removed by M. Appert, whose main purpose is to see their use by all consumers, and so ensure that it is more useful to his country.

Your Committee has often appreciated the selflessness of M. Appert, and his longstanding and constant concern to improve upon his early work; it therefore accordingly approves of the honour he has paid the Society by offering to place a copy of his book in its library, and it renders its thanks to the author.[284]

As 1832 began, Nicolas was continuing to find himself in financial difficulties. No doubt he received a reasonable return on his book, and sales of Appert goods must have been at least satisfactory. However, the costs of his factory continued to eat up any income with an insatiable appetite. Nicolas decided to try again to secure an allowance, or pension, from the government. Perhaps he also had his eye on his future and was possibly considering retirement at last now that he was 82 years old.

On Monday 23 January 1832 Nicolas wrote to the Minister of Trade and Public Works.[285] He had powerful support from the Advisory Council of Arts and Manufacturing, who in their meeting of 2 June 1832 proposed that Nicolas should receive 6,000 *francs*.[286] The Minister, by an order of 23 June 1832, awarded Nicolas a 3,000 *francs* allowance "as an encouragement for the services you have rendered to industry."[287]

Perhaps encouraged by this success, Nicolas submitted a request to the same minister, on Bastille Day, Saturday 14 July 1832, asking to be awarded the coveted *Légion d'Honneur* medal. Nicolas's request had an accompanying letter of support from Captain Louis-Claude de Saulces de Freycinet. We last met the Captain when, following his circumnavigation, he wrote a letter in 1822 to the Society for the Encouragement of National Industry, and an official report for the Navy Command, both endorsing the quality of Nicolas's preserves from his experiences on his three year voyage.

To *Monsieur le Ministre du Commerce et des Travaux Publics*, Captain De Freycinet wrote:

> Nobody has rendered sailors a more prominent and useful service than M. Appert, by the wonderful invention of canned food. Navigators from every navy in Europe have adopted these means and continue to report their immense advantages. It seems that the cross of the *Légion d'Honneur* cannot be placed on the chest of a more deserving man, who has sacrificed his long career and his fortune to improve the lives of a considerable part of society. For these reasons, I urge the Minister of Trade and Public Works to welcome and look kindly upon the above request of M. Appert.[288]

The *Légion d'Honneur* is France's highest decoration and is awarded at five levels. It was instituted by Napoleon Bonaparte in 1802 and is still awarded today. The levels have changed name over the years. They are currently (from lowest to highest level): *Chevalier* (Knight), *Officier*

(Officer), *Commandeur* (Commander), *Grand Officier* (Grand Officer) and *Grand-Croix* (Grand Cross). Under King Louis Philippe there were about 45,000 members, awarded for gallantry in action or twenty years' distinguished service in military or civilian life.

Unhappily, Nicolas did not receive this award. Perhaps his timing was poor, as Paris was in the grip of a cholera epidemic which started in March 1832 and over the ensuing six months claimed the lives of more than 18,400 Parisians. Most wealthy Parisians fled the city but the Royal Family and the government stayed. The Prime Minister, Casimir Périer, caught the disease while visiting the sick in hospital and died five weeks later. The Minister of Trade and Public Works may have had other things on his mind!

The following year, on Monday 29 April 1833, Nicolas's estranged wife, Elisabeth, died aged 74 at Neuilly-sur-Seine, just north of the *Bois de Boulogne*.[289] Now a suburb of Paris, Neuilly is about 2 miles further west than *rue Duras*, where Elisabeth had been living in the 1820s, and so about 4 miles west of Nicolas's premises in the *rue du Paradis*.

A few months later, on Saturday 6 July 1833, their daughter Amélie-Justine got married for the second time, five years after her first husband Jean-Louis Lefébure died in Guadeloupe. She married César Antoine Denis Graingault in Paris.[290] At some time in the next ten years Amélie-Justine and César moved to St. Julien de Civry, Saône et Loire, a small village, now of about 500 inhabitants, about 230 miles south east of Paris, on the road to Lyons.

Just two years after Elisabeth Appert, *née* Benoist, died, her sister Nicole-Sophie died. She was the widow of Nicolas's brother Jean-Baptiste, who had died in 1822. Nicole-Sophie died not long before her 72nd birthday in *l'hospice Saint-Maur* in Châlons-sur-Marne in February 1835.[291]

Commemorative First Day Cover Envelope
5 March 1955

(From the Author's collection)

Above: Note the incorrect date of Nicolas's death

Below: Detail from the reverse of the envelope
(now with correct death date!)

Nicolas may well have been in the crowds in what is now the *place de la Concorde* as the great obelisk of Rameses II from Luxor was erected on Tuesday 25 October 1836. This gift from the Pasha of Egypt, Mehmet Ali, still stands today. When Nicolas first moved to Paris this *place* had been named *place Louis XV*. It had been renamed the *place de la Révolution* by the time Nicolas witnessed the death of King Louis XVI there in January 1793. In 1795 the Directory changed the name to *place de la Concorde* to indicate reconciliation and peace. At the Restoration of the Monarchy in 1814 it reverted to *place Louis XV*, and then following the July Revolution in 1830 it was renamed again, *place Louis XVI*. Later, during the Empire, it became *place de Chartre*, before finally settling back to *place de la Concorde*.

Few places could reflect so clearly the upheavals and changes Nicolas had seen in his years in Paris. But now, as Nicolas approached his 87th birthday, he decided it was time to consider retirement.[292] He left his business to a relative, Claude-Auguste Prieur-Appert, and left Paris. In 1836 he returned to Massy where he and his family had spent their happiest years twenty to thirty years before.

The house on the left is
Nicolas Appert's last house

99 *rue de Paris/Grande Rue, Massy*

now a pharmacy on the corner of
rue Fustel de Coulanges and *rue Gabriel Péri*

Chapter 12

Last Days in Massy: 1836 – 1841

Nicolas first lived in part of the building he had sold in 1816, but then moved to smaller accommodation at 99 *rue de Paris*, otherwise known as *Grande Rue*, at the corner with the *rue du Cheval Blanc*, now called the *rue Fustel de Coulanges*.[293] His government pension by this time was 1,200 *francs*, reduced from the original award of 3,000 *francs*.[294] Joséphine Faillet is recorded as living at the same address – possibly Nicolas's servant or housekeeper.[295]

Nicolas must have spent quiet days walking in the fields that he knew so well. He would have heard, with pleasure, that Prieur-Appert had matched his success in being awarded a gold medal in the Paris Exposition of 1839 for his "appertised" products.

After four or five years of quiet retirement, Nicolas died at 8pm on Tuesday 1 June 1841 amid violent thunder storms.[296] The next day, the Mayor wrote:

> 2 June 1841, 10 o'clock in the morning, death certificate of Nicolas Appert, pensioner, aged 91 years, born in Châlons (Marne), who died yesterday at 8 o'clock in the evening in his home, *Grande Rue*, legitimate son of deceased Claude Appert and Marie Huet; widower of Elisabeth Benoist. The witnesses were M. Charles Lecomte, householder aged 50 years, and M. Alexis Saunier, householder aged 44 years, both neighbours of the deceased, who have signed this record of the death with us.

Signatures of: the Mayor, Lecomte and Saunier.[297]

L'Église Sainte Marie Madeleine, Massy
Old postcard showing the church where
Nicolas Appert was buried in 1841.
All but the tower was destroyed
in the Second World War.

(From the author's collection)

Nicolas was buried on the next day in the common grave[298] at *L'Église Sainte Marie Madeleine.* The entry in the *Registre des Baptêmes, mariages, sépultures de la pariosse de Massy* reads:

> Thursday 3 June 1841 was buried by us, *curé,* with church ceremonies the body of Nicolas Appert, aged 91 years, deceased in his home on *Grande Rue,* in the presence of the undersigned.

> Giboutet, priest of Massy[299]

The tower of *L'Église Sainte Marie Madeleine, Massy*

Just in front of the tower is the bust of Appert,
shown on the next page

221

Bronze bust in the grounds of
L'Église Sainte Marie Madeleine at Massy

By Richard Bruyère (1953 –)
Erected in 1999

Bronze bust as opposite

Being buried in the common grave would imply that Nicolas did not leave behind enough money for a separate burial. I think that this was probably not uncommon at the time, but it nevertheless ends his life on a sad note. He had changed so many lives for the better by his hard work and dedication, but the world let him leave without any special mark or thanks. It is not known whether any of his family was present at his funeral. I like to think that some were

223

there, perhaps his son Charles-Pierre-Nicolas, since he was living in Paris and might have got there in time.

A plaque (shown opposite) was erected in 1999, on the 250th anniversary of Nicolas's birth, on the wall of the house where he died.

The Society for the Encouragement of National Industry, which had meant so much to Nicolas over the years because of the support its members had given him, marked his passing at their meeting on Wednesday 16 June 1841:

> M. Chevallier announced that M. Appert, who discovered the art of preserving foodstuffs, has just died at an advanced age. The President [Louis Jacques Thénard] gave a presentation of the work of this industrialist who has given birth to several developments of great value to the domestic economy and to voyages of long duration.[300]

M. Prieur-Appert could well have been present at this meeting as he had been made a member of the Society two years before. Having already proved himself a worthy successor to Nicolas by his gold medal at the 1839 Exposition, he also revised Nicolas's book: *Le Livre de Tous les Ménages*, 5th edition, revised by MM. Prieur-Appert and Gannal, and published in Paris by E. Dentu in 1842.

Commemorative plaque
on the wall of Nicolas Appert's last house:

"NICOLAS APPERT
1749 – 1841

Chemist, inventor of the process
universally adopted for preserving
food in cans.

Lived and worked on his discovery
until his death at Massy, in these buildings."

Bronze medallion
by Boris Bernstein
(weight 207g, diameter 68mm, thickness 5mm)

(From the author's collection)

Reverse of the Bronze Medallion opposite

(From the author's collection)

Portrait of Nicolas Appert

Believed to be the only image taken during his lifetime.

Engraving by Auguste II Blanchard (1792 – 1849)[301]

Epilogue

At the time of Nicolas's death, his daughter Amélie-Justine and her second husband César were living in St. Julien de Civry, Saône et Loire. Two years later, Amélie-Justine's daughter, Céline Edmée Lefébure, married François Joseph Chabal on 8 August 1843, just before the bride's 21st birthday.[302]

François, a 39 year old widower, was a music editor and publisher, with premises at *N° 10 Boulevard des Italiens*, one of the four main *boulevards* of Paris and in the 19th century identified with Parisian style and fashion. In January 1841 François had published a first edition of Frédéric Chopin's *Mazourka pour le piano* in A minor, Opus 43, dedicated to Emile Gaillard, selling at 4 *francs* 50. In the catalogue of Chopin's complete works, this work has the annotation MEG-1-CH, the CH standing for Chabal.

Céline taught piano and so it may well have been through this that these two musical people met. After their marriage, they lived at *N° 10 rue Penon* in Paris. It was there that their first child, Ernest Jules Chabal, was born on 8 October 1844. Céline's mother, Amélie-Justine, died on Thursday 13 December 1855 in St. Julien de Civry.

Ernest Jules Chabal, my wife's great grandfather, worked as an engineer for a company called GM, and then for the *Compagnie des chemins de fer de Paris à Lyon et à la Méditerranée*, a major French railway company called PLM for short. Ernest became Chief Engineer, then Director of the company.

PLM ran the main line services from Paris to the south-east of France, and also the railway network in Algeria. In 1938 it was absorbed into the new national rail network SNCF, becoming the south-eastern region of the network.

For his services to France in the capacity of Director of PLM, Ernest Jules was awarded the honour that his great grandfather Nicolas had sought but did not receive: the *Légion d'Honneur*.

On 28 August 1877 Ernest Jules, aged 32, married 24 year old Clémence Eugenie Ronce in Sartrouville, Seine et Oise, about 10 miles north-west of central Paris. Clémence had been born on 14 January 1853 in the *rue de la Harpe*, Paris, just off the *Boulevard Saint-Germain*. They had three children: Pauline Alice Juliette Chabal, known in the family as Juliette, born on 7 February 1882 in Sartrouville, and two sons.

Juliette Chabal is my wife's grandmother. Juliette married Henri Chaudoye on 11 November 1903 and over the next 25 years they had twelve children. The tenth was Gilberte Monique Jeanne Chaudoye, born in Nantes on 11 March 1925.

Gilberte married Harold Andrews, who had been born in Devizes in Wiltshire, England, in May 1920. They lived from their marriage in August 1953 in Southampton. It was in Southampton that their two sons and two daughters were born, including of course my wife Cathy – or Catherine as she is known in the family.

Cathy knew her grandmother, Juliette Chaudoye, née Chabal, who died on Tuesday 19 January 1971, aged 88.

Juliette had known her grandmother, Céline Edmée Chabal, née Lefébure, who had died when Juliette was 10 years old.

Céline Edmée had known her grandfather, Nicolas Appert, who had died when Céline was aged 18.

These six generations separate Nicolas Appert from the present.

Among the changes that have taken place over those six generations there are many that would vie for the title of the most important or significant. I think that a strong case could be made for the unassuming tin can containing all the goodness of fresh food yet preserved until needed.

2010 marked the two hundredth anniversary of the publication of Nicolas's book, making known to the world the process of preserving food. This invention, which has helped countless people on the planet since, places Nicolas Appert in the forefront of inventors and of those individuals whose lives have had the most beneficial influence on posterity.

Family Tree

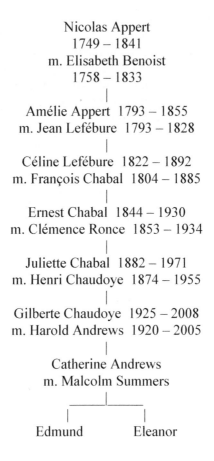

Nicolas Appert
1749 – 1841
m. Elisabeth Benoist
1758 – 1833
|
Amélie Appert 1793 – 1855
m. Jean Lefébure 1793 – 1828
|
Céline Lefébure 1822 – 1892
m. François Chabal 1804 – 1885
|
Ernest Chabal 1844 – 1930
m. Clémence Ronce 1853 – 1934
|
Juliette Chabal 1882 – 1971
m. Henri Chaudoye 1874 – 1955
|
Gilberte Chaudoye 1925 – 2008
m. Harold Andrews 1920 – 2005
|
Catherine Andrews
m. Malcolm Summers
|
Edmund   Eleanor

Endnotes & Sources

[1] *"Les Artisans Illustres"* by Édouard Foucaud, Paris 1841, page 630. The image used is in the public domain, downloaded from http://en.wikipedia.org/wiki/File:Appert_Nicolas.jpg (Accessed December 2013)

[2] *"Bulletin de la Société d'encouragement pour l'industrie national"* Volume 40 Paris 1841, p305

[3] http://archives.marne.fr *Baptêmes, mariages, sépultures* 1620-1771 Saint-Jean Châlons-en-Champagne (Accessed December 2013) Nicolas Appert – Baptism 17 November 1749

[4] A François Huet (1658-?) was an innkeeper in the St. John area in 1692. Cited in "Nicolas Appert" by Jean-Paul Barbier 1994 Royer, p16

[5] http://archives.marne.fr *Baptêmes, mariages, sépultures* 1620-1771 Saint-Jean Châlons-en-Champagne (Accessed December 2013) Marie-Nicolle Huet – Baptism 7 July 1714

[6] Nicolas's grandfather François Huet died in 1725 and his grandmother Marie Bertault died in 1736. http://archives.marne.fr *Baptêmes, mariages, sépultures* 1620-1771 Saint-Jean Châlons-en-Champagne (Accessed December 2013) François – Burial 21 September 1725 aged 33; Marie – Burial 2 January 1736 aged 46

[7] *Archives départementales de la Marne*, Cote 4E 6835 24.10.1739. Cited in "Nicolas Appert" by Jean-Paul Barbier 1994 Royer, p16 and in note 9 on p32

[8] http://archives.marne.fr *Baptêmes, mariages, sépultures* 1620-1771 Saint-Jean (Accessed December 2013) Marriage 9 November 1739

[9] http://archives.marne.fr *Baptêmes, mariages, sépultures* 1732 – 1747 Saint-Jean (Accessed December 2014) Claude is given as aged 28 at his marriage to Marie Nicolle Huet on 9 November 1739

[10] "Nicolas Appert" by Jean-Paul Barbier 1994 Royer, p14

[11] *"Elevée vers 1100 la nef de l'église Saint-Jean est le plus ancien monument de Châlons-en-Champagne"* Tourist Information Leaflet, Office de Tourisme, 3 Quai des Artes, 51000 Châlons-en-Champagne

[12] Downloaded from http://commons.wikimedia.org/wiki/File:Église_st-Jean_et_auberge_cheval_blanc_Appert_par_Leblanc_1792.jpg (Accessed January 2014). Image allowed for use by terms of licence of the copyright holder G. Garitan

[13] http://www.populstat.info/Europe/francet.htm (Accessed December 2013)

[14] "The Fifteen Decisive Battles of the World" by Sir Edward Shepherd Creasy M.A., 1851, Chapters VI and XIV

[15] Louis-Gervais Appert born 19 October 1740, died 10 May 1809. For his baptism see http://archives.marne.fr *Baptêmes, mariages, sépultures* 1620-1771 Saint-Jean Châlons-en-Champagne (Accessed December 2013). For his death see Note 173 below

[16] Marie-Anne Appert born 26 December 1741, died 9 January 1748. For her baptism see http://archives.marne.fr *Baptêmes, mariages, sépultures* 1620-1771 Saint-Jean Châlons-en-Champagne (Accessed December 2013). For her death see http://archives.marne.fr *Baptêmes, mariages, sépultures* 1748 – 1758 Saint-Jean Châlons-en-Champagne (Accessed December 2014)

[17] Twins Augustin and Margueritte Appert were born on 22 April 1743. Both died as infants. For their baptisms see http://archives.marne.fr *Baptêmes, mariages, sépultures* 1732-1747 Saint-Jean Châlons-en-Champagne (Accessed December 2013). For Augustin's death, see "Nicolas Appert" by Jean-Paul Barbier 1994 Royer, p32, note 12. Barbier was incorrect about Margueritte's death – see his note p32 note 12 – confusing her with her sister Marie-Margueritte

[18] Marie-Margueritte Appert was born 13 November 1744 and died 24 October 1760. For her baptism, see http://archives.marne.fr *Baptêmes, mariages, sépultures* 1620-1771 Saint-Jean Châlons-en-Champagne (Accessed December 2013) For her death see http://archives.marne.fr *Baptêmes, mariages, sépultures* 1755-1770 Notre Dame Châlons-en-Champagne (Accessed December 2013)

[19] Jules-Claude-Marie Appert was born on 10 January 1746 and died on 30 April 1825. For his baptism see http://archives.marne.fr *Baptêmes, mariages, sépultures* 1620-1771 Saint-Jean Châlons-en-Champagne (Accessed December 2013). For his death see "Nicolas Appert" by Jean-Paul Barbier 1994 Royer, p32, note 14

[20] Louis-Etienne Appert was born on 3 Mar 1747 and died in infancy. For his baptism see http://archives.marne.fr *Baptêmes, mariages, sépultures* 1620-1771 Saint-Jean Châlons-en-Champagne (Accessed December 2013). For his death see "Nicolas Appert" by Jean-Paul Barbier 1994 Royer, p32, note 15

[21] Marie-Reine Appert was born on 7 April 1748 and died on 22 August 1754. For her baptism see http://archives.marne.fr *Baptêmes, mariages, sépultures* 1620-1771 Saint-Jean Châlons-en-Champagne (Accessed December 2013). For her death see "Nicolas Appert" by Jean-Paul Barbier 1994 Royer, p32, note 16

[22] Image used from http://jean-paul.barbier.perso.sfr.fr/ gene.html (Accessed December 2013). *Archives départementales de la Marne*, Cote 2 E 119/21 Saint-Jean Châlons; http://archives.marne.fr *Baptêmes,*

mariages, sépultures 1748 – 1758 Saint-Jean, Châlons (Accessed December 2013) Nicolas Appert - Baptism 17 November 1749

[23] http://jean-paul.barbier.perso.sfr.fr/gene.html (Accessed December 2013), *Le Musée, La Salle: Acte de Baptême*

[24] See Note 29 below for details

[25] *Archives départementales de la Marne*, Cote 4E 1068. Cited in "Nicolas Appert" by Jean-Paul Barbier 1994 Royer, p18 and in note 17 on p32

[26] François Appert was born 30 December 1750. For his baptism on 1 January 1751 see http://archives.marne.fr *Baptêmes, mariages, sépultures* 1730 – 1754 Notre-Dame, Châlons-en-Champagne (Accessed December 2013)

[27] "Nicolas Appert" by Jean-Paul Barbier 1994 Royer, p32, note 17

[28] Claude Appert died on 27 July 1780 and was buried two days later. See http://archives.marne.fr *Baptêmes, mariages, sépultures* 1620 – 1785 Notre-Dame (Accessed December 2013)

[29] Jean-Baptiste born 16 May 1752 and baptised the following day. See http://archives.marne.fr *Baptêmes, mariages, sépultures* 1730 – 1754 Notre-Dame (Accessed December 2013)

[30] François Huet born 12 July 1715. For his baptism see http://archives.marne.fr *Baptêmes, mariages, sépultures* 1620-1771 Saint-Jean Châlons-en-Champagne (Accessed December 2013)

[31] See note 21 above. Also "Nicolas Appert" by Jean-Paul Barbier 1994 Royer, p23

[32] See note 18 above

[33] "Nicolas Appert" by Jean-Paul Barbier 1994 Royer, p22

[34] "The Art of Preserving Animal and Vegetable Substances for Many Years" by Nicolas Appert 1810, translation by K. G. Bitting, Chicago 1920, p6

[35] "*L'art de conserver pendant plusieurs années toutes les substances animales et végétales*" by Nicolas Appert, 1831 Barros 3rd Edition, p138

[36] Image used is in the public domain, downloaded from http://en.wikipedia.org/wiki/File:Stanislaw_Leszczynski.jpg (Accessed December 2013)

[37] *Archives départementales de la Marne*, Cote 4E 4437 Purchase from Louis Clément. Cited in "Nicolas Appert" by Jean-Paul Barbier 1994 Royer, p28 and in note 29 p34

[38] "Nicolas Appert" by Jean-Paul Barbier 1994 Royer, p32f, note 17. See also *Archives départementales de la Marne*, Cote 1L 194

[39] *Archives départementales de la Marne*, Cote C438. Cited in "Nicolas Appert" by Jean-Paul Barbier 1994 Royer, p28 and note 31 on p34

[40] Image used from http://www.holocaustianity.com /zweibruckener.html (Accessed May 2014)

[41] Image used is in the public domain, from a painting by Johann Christian von Mannlich. Downloaded from http://en.wikipedia.org/wiki/File: Christian_IV_of_Palatinate-Zweibrücken.jpg (Accessed December 2013)

[42] Information given on the title page of "*L'art de conserver pendant plusieurs années toutes les substances animales et végétales*" by Nicolas Appert, Paris 1810. Also "Nicolas Appert" by Jean-Paul Barbier 1994 Royer, p29

[43] The marriage of Jules-Claude-Marie Appert and Jeanne-Catherine Lamairesse at Coolus, see http://archives.marne.fr *Baptêmes, mariages, sépultures* 1695 – 1792 Coolus Cote 2E 189/1 7 September 1773 (Accessed December 2013). Nicolas is named, together with his father Claude and Uncle Nicolas, as witnesses to the marriage

[44] *Archives départementales de la Marne*, Cote 4E 8310, cited in "Nicolas Appert" by Jean-Paul Barbier 1994 Royer, p29 and note 34 on p34

[45] Image used was downloaded from http://www.un-forbachois.net (Accessed September 2008)

[46] "Nicolas Appert" by Jean-Paul Barbier 1994 Royer, p29

[47] http://franklinpapers.org (Accessed December 2013)

[48] François, Appert was buried on 1 October 1778. See http://archives.marne.fr *Baptêmes, mariages, sépultures* 1620 – 1785 Notre-Dame, Châlons Cote 2E 788/2 (Accessed December 2013)

[49] "Nicolas Appert" by Jean-Paul Barbier 1994 Royer, p30

[50] *Archives départementales de la Marne*, Cote 2E 119/3 Notre-Dame-en-Vaux, Châlons-en-Champagne. See Note 28 above.

[51] *Archives départementales de la Marne*, Cote B 122, cited in "Nicolas Appert" by Jean-Paul Barbier 1994 Royer, p30 and note 37 on p34

[52] http://en.wikisource.org/wiki/1911_Encyclopædia_Britannica/Appert_Benjamin_Nicolas_Marie (Accessed December 2013)

[53] *Encyclopédie des gens du monde, répertoire universel des sciences, des lettres et des arts : avec des notices sur les principales familles historiques et sur les personnages célèbres, morts et vivans* Volume 2 1833 Paris, p106

[54] *Archives Nationales* F7 4580, cited in "Nicolas Appert" by Jean-Paul Barbier 1994 Royer, p37 and note 3 on p68

[55] *Archives départementales de la Seine*, N 794. Also detailed in *Archives départementales de l'Essonne* 4E 1941, on the entry for his daughter Amélie Justine's marriage in March 1815

[56] Elisabeth Benoist was born on 11 July 1758. For her baptism see http://archives.marne.fr *Baptêmes, mariages, sépultures* 1755 – 1760 2 E 534/130 Saint-Pierre Reims (Accessed December 2013)

[57] "Nicolas Appert" by Jean-Paul Barbier 1994 Royer, p37 and note 6 on p68; death dates from research by Arnold Schuller

[58] *Archives Nationales* F7 4798 folio 136, cited in "Nicolas Appert" by Jean-Paul Barbier 1994 Royer, p37 and note 4 on p68

[59] Charles Pierre Nicolas Appert born 27 May 1786 baptised at *L'église Saint-Jacques Le Majeur*. For his baptism see http://canadp-archivesenligne.paris.fr/archives_etat_civil/ avant_1860 V3E/N 37

[60] Elisabeth-Marie-Nicole Appert born on 10 August 1787, baptised at *L'église Saint-Jacques Le Majeur*. For her baptism see http://canadp-archivesenligne.paris.fr/ archives_ etat_civil/avant_1860 V3E/N 37

[61] Aglaë-Françoise Appert born 5 January 1789, baptised at *L'église Saint-Jacques Le Majeur*. For her baptism see http://canadp-archivesenligne.paris.fr/archives_etat_civil/ avant_1860 V3E/N 37

[62] "Nicolas Appert" by Jean-Paul Barbier 1994 Royer, p40f

[63] *Archives départementales de la Marne*, Cote 4E 8317, cited in "Nicolas Appert" by Jean-Paul Barbier 1994 Royer, p37f and note 10 on p69

[64] "Nicolas Appert" by Jean-Paul Barbier 1994 Royer, p38

[65] Nicole-Sophie Benoist was born on 2 March 1763 in Reims. See *Archives départementales de la Marne* Cote 4E 1639; for the marriage of Jean-Baptiste and Nicole-Sophie, see *Archives nationales Minutier Central* ET CX 528, ET IX 886, cited in "Nicolas Appert" by Jean-Paul Barbier 1994 Royer, note 12 on p69

[66] "Nicolas Appert" by Jean-Paul Barbier 1994 Royer. p42

[67] Ibid.

[68] "The French Revolution", Christopher Hibbard, Penguin 1982, p82f

[69] http://www.archivesnationales.culture.gouv.fr/chan/chan/pdf/sm/F1dII 29-32%201%20VainqBastille.pdf (Accessed December 2013)

[70] Image used is in the public domain. Downloaded in December 2013 from http://en. wikipedia.org/wiki/File: Prise_de_la_Bastille.jpg

[71] "Nicolas Appert" by Jean-Paul Barbier 1994 Royer, p42

[72] *Archives départementales de la Marne* Cote 4E 8317, cited in "Nicolas Appert" by Jean-Paul Barbier 1994 Royer, p42 and note 19 on p70

[73] Marie-Nicolle Huet died on 16 January 1790. Burial entry, signed by sons Claude Appert, *marchand et epicier*, and Jean Appert, at http://archives.marne.fr *Baptêmes, mariages, sépultures* 1782 – 1792 Notre-Dame, Châlons Cote 2E 119/4 (Accessed December 2013). Burial 18 January 1790

[74] *Archives départementales de la Marne* Cote 4E 15382, cited in "Nicolas Appert" by Jean-Paul Barbier 1994 Royer, p43 and note 22 on p70

[75] "Nicolas Appert" by Jean-Paul Barbier 1994 Royer, p43

[76]Ibid. p44; note 26 on p70 cites that *Archives de la Préfecture de Police à Paris* AA163 10 March 1793 refers to "*Appert Commissaire à la commission de la guerre.*"

[77] "Nicolas Appert" by Jean-Paul Barbier 1994 Royer, p44

[78] Ibid. p42

[79] Ibid. p45

[80] *Archives nationales* F7 4580, cited in "Nicolas Appert" by Jean-Paul Barbier 1994 Royer, p45 and note 30 on p71

[81] "Nicolas Appert" by Jean-Paul Barbier 1994 Royer, p45

[82] Image used is in the public domain. Downloaded from http://en.wikipedia.org/wiki/File:Valmy_Battle_painting.jpg (Accessed December 2013)

[83] *Archives départementales de la Seine* Cote 1AZ 159 *Section des Lombards*, cited in "Nicolas Appert" by Jean-Paul Barbier 1994 Royer, p46 and note 35 on p72

[84] "Nicolas Appert" by Jean-Paul Barbier 1994 Royer, p42

[85] *"Rapport des citoyens Poullenot et Joly, commissaires de la section des Lombards, au bataillon de cette section, à l'armée de Dumourier, fait en la séance du 10 octobre 1792"* Limodin, Paris 1792

[86] *Le Moniteur Universel* No. 290, *Mardi 16 Octobre 1792*; online at https://archive.org/stream/rimpressiondela11univgoog#page/n241/mode/2 up (Accessed Decemeber 2013)

[87] "Nicolas Appert" by Jean-Paul Barbier 1994 Royer, p50

[88] Ibid.

[89] *Archives de la Préfecture de Police à Paris* AA163 10 March 1793, cited in "Nicolas Appert" by Jean-Paul Barbier 1994 Royer, p50 and note 44 on p72

[90] Image used is in the public domain. Downloaded from http://en.wikipedia.org/wiki/File:Execution_of_Louis_XVI.jpg (Accessed December 2013)

[91] Donation on 15 May 1793, "Nicolas Appert" by Jean-Paul Barbier 1994 Royer, p52

[92] "Nicolas Appert" by Jean-Paul Barbier 1994 Royer, p52

[93] *Archives nationales* C 252 No. 442, cited in "Nicolas Appert" by Jean-Paul Barbier 1994 Royer, p52 and note 47 on p73

[94] *Archives nationales* BB3 74, cited in "Nicolas Appert" by Jean-Paul Barbier 1994 Royer, p53, and note 49 on p73

[95] *Archives nationales* F7 4580, cited in "Nicolas Appert" by Jean-Paul Barbier 1994 Royer, p54 and note 50 p73

[96] Image used is in the public domain. Downloaded from http://en.wikipedia.org/wiki /File:Robespierre.jpg (Accessed December 2013)

[97] "Nicolas Appert" by Jean-Paul Barbier 1994 Royer, p54

[98] *Archives nationales* F7 4774/24, cited in "Nicolas Appert" by Jean-Paul Barbier 1994 Royer, p55 and note 52 on p73

[99] *Archives nationales* F7 4580, also *Le rigistre de la section des Amis de La Patrie Archives Nationales* F7 2489, cited in "Nicolas Appert" by Jean-Paul Barbier 1994 Royer, p55 and note 53 on p73

[100] *Archives Nationales* F7 4785, cited in "Nicolas Appert" by Jean-Paul Barbier 1994 Royer, p56 and note 54 on p73

[101] Amélie-Justine Appert was born on 23 July 1793. See http://canadp-archivesenligne.paris.fr/archives_etat_civil/ avant_1860 V3E/N 37 ; details also given on her marriage certificate *Archives Départementales de l'Essonne* 4E 1941, http://www.archinoe.net Massy 1809-1815 (Accessed April 2014)

[102] "Nicolas Appert" by Jean-Paul Barbier 1994 Royer, p56

[103] Ibid.

[104] Ibid. p57

[105] Ibid. p58

[106] Ibid.

[107] Ibid.

[108] Ibid. p59

[109] *Archives Nationales* F7 4580, cited in "Nicolas Appert" by Jean-Paul Barbier 1994 Royer, p59 and note 64 on p75

[110] Image used is in public domain. Downloaded from http://commons.wikimedia.org/wiki/File:Boilly_Prison_des_Madelonnettes,_1805.png (Accessed December 2013)

[111] "Nicolas Appert" by Jean-Paul Barbier 1994 Royer, p64f

[112] Ibid. p66

[113] *Archives Nationales* F7 4580, cited in "Nicolas Appert" by Jean-Paul Barbier 1994 Royer, p51 (with an incorrect date), p67 and note 71 on p76

[114] *"Rapports du Jury sur L'Exposition Universelle Internationale de 1889"* Paris 1891, p90 ; online at http://cnum.cnam.fr/CGI/fpage.cgi?8XAE348.17/94/100/505/0/0 (Accessed December 2013)

[115] *Archives Nationales* F7 2493, cited in "Nicolas Appert" by Jean-Paul Barbier 1994 Royer, p67 and note 73 on p76

[116] "Nicolas Appert" by Jean-Paul Barbier 1994 Royer, p55 and Note 57 on p74

[117] *Archives Municipales Ivry-sur-Seine Etat des élections an IX,* cited in "Nicolas Appert" by Jean-Paul Barbier 1994 Royer, p79 and note 2 on p107

[118] 1765 plan courtesy of the staff at the Archives at the *Mairie d'Ivry, Esplanade Georges Marrane, 94200 Ivry-sur-Seine* (visited October 2014)

[119] *14 germinal an III* (3 April 1795) *Archives départementales de la Marne*, Cote 4E 8323, cited in "Nicolas Appert" by Jean-Paul Barbier 1994 Royer, p79 and note 3 on p107

[120] *Archives Municipales Ivry-sur-Seine Registre des déliberations* 1 D1/3, with thanks to the Archive staff at the *Mairie d'Ivry-sur-Seine* (visited October 2014)

[121] Appert missed only the meetings of *21 et 23 fructidor an III* (7 and 9 September 1795) and *25 et 30 brumaire an IV* (16 and 21 November 1795), cited in "Nicolas Appert" by Jean-Paul Barbier 1994 Royer, p80

[122] *Municipales Ivry-sur-Seine Registre des déliberations* 1 D1/3, with thanks to the Archive staff at the *Mairie d'Ivry-sur-Seine* (visited October 2014)

[123] *Archives départementales du Val de Marne, Naissances, mariages, décès* 1791 – 1795 Cote 1MI 151; online at http://archives.cg94.fr /consultation/eta/img-viewer/etat-civil/94041/1MI_000151/viewer.html p235 (Accessed December 2013)

[124] Ibid. p214

[125] *Archives départementales de la Seine* D5 B6 No. 6002, cited in "Nicolas Appert" by Jean-Paul Barbier 1994 Royer, p84 and note 14 on p107

[126] "The Art of Preserving All Kinds of Animal and Vegetable Substances for Several Years" by Nicolas Appert, 1812 London (translation of 1810 edition) p132ff; in the Paris 1810 original French edition p102ff

[127] *"Le Livre de Tous Les Ménages ou L'Art de Conserver, pendant plusieurs années, toutes les substances animales et végétales"* by Nicolas Appert, Paris 1810 p1

[128] Ibid. p6

[129] *"Le Livre de Tous Les Ménages ou L'Art de Conserver, pendant plusieurs années, toutes les substances animales et végétales"* by Nicolas Appert, Paris 3rd Edition 1813 p xvi, which repeated his foreword from his 2nd Edition of 1811

[130] *"Le Livre de Tous Les Ménages ou L'Art de Conserver, pendant plusieurs années, toutes les substances animales et végétales"* by Nicolas Appert, Paris 1810 p90

[131] Ibid. p8f

[132] "Nicolas Appert" by Jean-Paul Barbier 1994 Royer, p81f

[133] *"Le Livre de Tous Les Ménages ou L'Art de Conserver, pendant plusieurs années, toutes les substances animales et végétales"* by Nicolas Appert, Paris 1831 p xvij footnote (1)

[134] Trade Directory for Year 8 (1799-1800), cited in "Nicolas Appert" by Jean-Paul Barbier 1994 Royer, p82

[135] *"Documents du Minutier central des notaires de Paris concernant l'histoire économique et sociale (1800 – 1830)"* by Andrée Chauleur, Paris *Centre historique des Archives nationales* 1999, p369 (Item 3795)

[136] http://fr.topic-topos.com/centre-saint-exupery-massy (Accessed January 2014); also "Nicolas Appert" by Jean-Paul Barbier 1994 Royer, p88

[137] *Archives départementales de l'Essonne* 1811, reproduced in "Nicolas Appert" by Rosamonde Pujol, Denoël 1985 p95

[138] "The Art of Preserving All Kinds of Animal and Vegetable Substances for Several Years" by Nicolas Appert, 1812 London (translation of 1810 edition) p11ff; in the Paris 1810 original French edition p9ff

[139] Although referring to Appert's 1810 edition, these images are from the author's own copy of the 1831 edition of Appert's book

[140] *"Le Livre de Tous Les Ménages ou L'Art de Conserver, pendant plusieurs années, toutes les substances animales et végétales"* by Nicolas Appert, Paris 1810 p106

[141] "Nicolas Appert" by Jean-Paul Barbier 1994 Royer, p91; also *Archives départementales de la Seine* D5 B6 No. 6002

[142] *"Le Livre de Tous Les Ménages ou L'Art de Conserver, pendant plusieurs années, toutes les substances animales et végétales"* by Nicolas Appert, Paris 1810 p xxiv

[143] Ibid. p43f

[144] *"L'Almanach des Gourmands"* by Grimod de la Reynière, Third Edition, Maradan of Paris 1805 p117

[145] Image used is in the public domain, downloaded from http://en.wikipedia.org/wiki/File:GrimodDeLAReyniere.jpg (Accessed January 2014)

[146] *"L'Almanach des Gourmands"* by Grimod de la Reynière, Third Edition, Maradan of Paris 1805 p135-136

[147] Ibid. p137-138

[148] Image from *"Le Livre de Tous Les Ménages ou L'Art de Conserver, pendant plusieurs années, toutes les substances animales et végétales"* by Nicolas Appert, Paris 1810. Image used is in the public domain, downloaded from http://commons.wikimedia.org/wiki/File:Nicolas_ Appert_Signature.svg (Accessed January 2014)

[149] *"L'Almanach des Gourmands"* by Grimod de la Reynière, Fourth Edition, Maradan of Paris 1806 p180

[150] *"L'Almanach des Gourmands"* by Grimod de la Reynière, Fifth Edition, Maradan of Paris 1807 p291-293

[151] *Archives départementales de la Seine* D11 U3 C33, cited in "Nicolas Appert" by Jean-Paul Barbier 1994 Royer, p97 and note 27 on p108

[152] Ibid.

[153] *Archives Nationales Minutier Central* ET/ XVI/ 970 dated 7 November 1807, cited in "Nicolas Appert" by Jean-Paul Barbier 1994 Royer, p98 and note 28 on p108

[154] *"L'Almanach des Gourmands"* by Grimod de la Reynière, Sixth Edition, Maradan of Paris 1808 p106

[155] "Nicolas Appert" by Jean-Paul Barbier 1994 Royer, p98

[156] Ibid. p99

[157] This trip is described with much invention and imagination in *"Nicolas Appert"* by Rosemonde Pujol, Denoël 1985, p110ff. The facts are given in *"L'Almanach des Gourmands"* by Grimod de la Reynière, Sixth Edition, Maradan of Paris 1808 p102-107

[158] *"Le Livre de Tous Les Ménages ou L'Art de Conserver, pendant plusieurs années, toutes les substances animales et végétales"* by Nicolas Appert, Paris 1810 p xxvi-xxvij

[159] Ibid. p xxiv-xxv

[160] Ibid. p xxvij-xxviij

[161] Ibid. p xxv

[162] *"L'Almanach des Gourmands"* by Grimod de la Reynière, Sixth Edition, Maradan of Paris 1808 p105 Footnote 1

[163] Ibid. p275

[164] *"Le Livre de Tous Les Ménages ou L'Art de Conserver, pendant plusieurs années, toutes les substances animales et végétales"* by Nicolas Appert, Paris 1831 p130-134

[165] *"Études sur le vin, ses maladies, causes qui les provoquent, procédés nouveaux pour le conserver et pour le vieillir"* by Louis Pasteur, Paris 1866 p80

[166] http://www.industrienationale.fr/wp-content/uploads/2007/12/plaquette 2007.pdf p2 and p9 (Accessed January 2014)

[167] *"Le Livre de Tous Les Ménages ou L'Art de Conserver, pendant plusieurs années, toutes les substances animales et végétales"* by Nicolas Appert, Paris 1813 p xxvij

[168] Ibid. p xxviij

[169] http://cnum.cnam.fr/CGI/fpage.cgi?BSPI.8/112/100/425/24/368 *"Bulletin de la Société d'Encouragement pour l'Industrie Nationale"* 8th Year No. 58 April 1809 p109ff (Accessed January 2014)

[170] *"Archives des Découvertes et des inventions nouvelles"* Paris 1809 p225ff

[171] *"Le Livre de Tous Les Ménages ou L'Art de Conserver, pendant plusieurs années, toutes les substances animales et végétales"* by Nicolas Appert, Paris 1810 p xvij – xxxij

[172] Ibid. p xv – xvj

[173] "Nicolas Appert" by Jean-Paul Barbier 1994 Royer, p32 Note 10

[174] *Archives nationales* F12 2432, cited in "Nicolas Appert" by Jean-Paul Barbier 1994 Royer, p115 and note 2 on p138

[175] *"Le Livre de Tous Les Ménages ou L'Art de Conserver, pendant plusieurs années, toutes les substances animales et végétales"* by Nicolas Appert, Paris 1831 p251-253

[176] Ibid. p250-251

[177] *"Le Livre de Tous Les Ménages ou L'Art de Conserver, pendant plusieurs années, toutes les substances animales et végétales"* by Nicolas Appert, Paris 1810 p5-6

[178] http://en.wikipedia.org/wiki/Nicolas_Appert (Accessed January 2014)

[179] *"Rapports du Jury sur L'Exposition Universelle Internationale de 1889"* Paris 1891, p90-91 ; online at http://cnum.cnam.fr/CGI/fpage.cgi?8XAE348.17/94/100/505/0/0 (Accessed January 2014)

[180] "Nicolas Appert" by Jean-Paul Barbier 1994 Royer, p118

[181] Ibid.

[182] *"Le Livre de Tous Les Ménages ou L'Art de Conserver, pendant plusieurs années, toutes les substances animales et végétales"* by Nicolas Appert, Paris 1831 p124-125

[183] "Nicolas Appert" by Jean-Paul Barbier 1994 Royer, p119

[184] *"Le Livre de Tous Les Ménages ou L'Art de Conserver, pendant plusieurs années, toutes les substances animales et végétales"* by Nicolas Appert, Paris 1810 p ix – xij (English translation from "The Art of Preserving All Kinds of Animal and Vegetable Substances for Several Years" by Nicolas Appert, 1812 London p xxi – xxiii)

[185] *"Le Livre de Tous Les Ménages ou L'Art de Conserver, pendant plusieurs années, toutes les substances animales et végétales"* by Nicolas Appert, Paris 1810 p xij – xiij (English translation from "The Art of Preserving All Kinds of Animal and Vegetable Substances for Several Years" by Nicolas Appert, 1812 London p xxiii – xxiv)

[186] "The Art of Preserving All Kinds of Animal and Vegetable Substances for Several Years" by Nicolas Appert, 1812 London p79

[187] *"Le Livre de Tous Les Ménages ou L'Art de Conserver, pendant plusieurs années, toutes les substances animales et végétales"* by Nicolas Appert, Paris 1813 p xxx

[188] Ibid. p xxix

[189] Ibid. p xxvij

[190] "Nicolas Appert" by Jean-Paul Barbier 1994 Royer, p122

[191] Ibid.

[192] "Nicolas Appert" by Rosamonde Pujol, Denoël 1985 p139-140

[193] *"Le Livre de Tous Les Ménages ou L'Art de Conserver, pendant plusieurs années, toutes les substances animales et végétales"* by Nicolas Appert, Paris 1813 p xxviij – xxix

[194] *Archives départementales de la Marne*, 99-1, cited in "Nicolas Appert" by Jean-Paul Barbier 1994 Royer, p128 and note 9 on p138

[195] *Archives Nationales* F12 2432, cited in "Nicolas Appert" by Jean-Paul Barbier 1994 Royer, p128 and note 10 on p138

[196] The full patent is reproduced in "Appertizing, or The Art of Canning, its history and development" by Arvill Wayne Bitting M.D., San Francisco 1937 p23f

[197] "The Repertory of Arts, Manufactures and Agriculture" No. CXII Second Series September 1811 collected in Volume XIX (Second Series) of the same title, London 1811 p195-196

[198] In "Food Packaging: Principles and Practice" by Gordon L. Robertson, Second Edition, Boca Raton, Florida 2006 p124, it states that Girard used Durand merely as a broker in London, and that it was Girard who sold the Patent to Donkin & Hall for £1,000

[199] *"Le Livre de Tous Les Ménages ou L'Art de Conserver, pendant plusieurs années, toutes les substances animales et végétales"* by Nicolas Appert, Paris 1813 p xxxi; also see "Nicolas Appert" by Jean-Paul Barbier 1994 Royer, p126

[200] *"Le Livre de Tous Les Ménages ou L'Art de Conserver, pendant plusieurs années, toutes les substances animales et végétales"* by Nicolas Appert, Paris 1810 p4, 7

[201] *"Le Livre de Tous Les Ménages ou L'Art de Conserver, pendant plusieurs années, toutes les substances animales et végétales"* by Nicolas Appert, Paris 1831 p xvij-xix footnote 2

[202] "The Morning Chronicle" published in London, Number 13,298 dated Saturday 21 December 1881, p1 column 4 "Books Published This Day"

[203] "The Art of Preserving All Kinds of Animal and Vegetable Substances for Several Years" by Nicolas Appert, 1812 London (translation of 1810 edition) p137 – 141; in the Paris 1810 original French edition p107 – 111

[204] *Archives Nationales* F12 2432, cited in "Nicolas Appert" by Jean-Paul Barbier 1994 Royer, p130 and note 14 on p138

[205] *Almanach des Gourmands*, Eighth year, Paris 1812 p70

[206] Ibid. p276f

[207] *Annuaire de l'Industrie française* No. 76, 1812; refuted by Nicolas in *"Le Livre de Tous Les Ménages ou L'Art de Conserver, pendant plusieurs années, toutes les substances animales et végétales"* by Nicolas Appert, Paris 1813 p iv - v

[208] Article *Conserves, etc, et autres* in *Journal d'Économie rurale et domestique, ou Bibliothèque des Propriétaires ruraux* April 1812 Issue No. 109 p63; refuted by Nicolas in *"Le Livre de Tous Les Ménages ou L'Art de Conserver, pendant plusieurs années, toutes les substances animales et végétales"* by Nicolas Appert, Paris 1813 p v

[209] *"Le Livre de Tous Les Ménages ou L'Art de Conserver, pendant plusieurs années, toutes les substances animales et végétales"* by Nicolas Appert, Paris 1813 p xxxi – xxxxvi (sic)

[210] *Archives Nationales minutier Central* ET/ XXI/ 724, cited in "Nicolas Appert" by Jean-Paul Barbier 1994 Royer p131 and in p138 footnote 19

[211] *"Le Livre de Tous Les Ménages ou L'Art de Conserver, pendant plusieurs années, toutes les substances animales et végétales"* by Nicolas Appert, Paris 1831 p ij; also see "Nicolas Appert" by Jean-Paul Barbier 1994 Royer, p134, which also quotes *Archives Nationales* F12 2432

[212] *"Bulletin de la Société d'Encouragement pour L'Industrie Nationale"* Paris 1814, p218 footnote 1

[213] Ibid. p219

[214] Ibid.

[215] *"Le Livre de Tous Les Ménages ou L'Art de Conserver, pendant plusieurs années, toutes les substances animales et végétales"* by Nicolas Appert, Paris 1831 p50

[216] "Nicolas Appert" by Jean-Paul Barbier 1994 Royer p136

[217] *Archives Départementales de l'Essonne* 4E 1941, http://www.archinoe.net Massy 1809-1815 (Accessed April 2014). Jean-Louis's father, Jean Lefébure, was born on 26 April 1753 in Pont-Farcy, Calvados, midway between Caen and St. Malo. Now a very small village of about 500 persons, Pont-Farcy was then a thriving river port on the River La Vire. Jean-Louis's mother, Marie Louise Calvastre, was born on 11 November 1752 in Maintenon in the Eure-et-Loire Department, some 40 miles south west of Paris. Maintenon is chiefly known for its lovely château, bought in 1674 by King Louis XIV's mistress and later secret second wife Françoise d'Aubigné, known as Madame de Maintenon.

[218] *"Le Livre de Tous Les Ménages ou L'Art de Conserver, pendant plusieurs années, toutes les substances animales et végétales"* by Nicolas Appert, Paris 1831 p46f

[219] *Archives Nationales* F12 2432 Letter written by Appert on 16 February 1825, cited in "Nicolas Appert" by Jean-Paul Barbier 1994 Royer p136, and note 23 on p139

[220] "Nicolas Appert" by Jean-Paul Barbier 1994 Royer p143

[221] *"Bulletin de la Société d'Encouragement pour l'Industrie Nationale"* Paris 1816 (15th Year) p240

[222] *Archives Nationales* F12 2432 Letter written by Appert on 16 February 1825, cited in "Nicolas Appert" by Jean-Paul Barbier 1994 Royer p144, and note 3 on p183

[223] *Archives Nationales* F12 2384, cited in "Nicolas Appert" by Jean-Paul Barbier 1994 Royer, p144 and note 5 on p183

[224] *"Bulletin de la Société d'Encouragement pour l'Industrie Nationale"* Paris 1817 (16th Year) p65

[225] "Nicolas Appert" by Jean-Paul Barbier 1994 Royer p144

[226] Image downloaded from http://commons.wikimedia.org/wiki/File: Hopital_des_Quinze-Vingt_1567_Paris.jpg from a 1900 postcard. This image is in the public domain. (Accessed April 2014)

[227] "Nicolas Appert" by Jean-Paul Barbier 1994 Royer p146

[228] *Archives Nationales* F12 2432 and cited in "Nicolas Appert" by Jean-Paul Barbier 1994 Royer p146

[229] *Archives Nationales Minutes du notaire Jean-Baptiste Mérault (étude CXI)* 1 July 1828, cited in "Nicolas Appert" by Jean-Paul Barbier 1994 Royer, p147 and note 10 on p183

[230] *"Annales de l'Agriculture Française" Deuxième Série Tome II*, Paris 1818 p101-105

[231] "Nicolas Appert" by Rosamonde Pujol, Denoël 1985 p176

[232] *"Bulletin de la Société d'Encouragement pour l'Industrie Nationale"* Paris 1819 (18th Year) p88

[233] "Nicolas Appert" by Jean-Paul Barbier 1994 Royer, note 22 on p184. Also see Note 229 above

[234] *"Bulletin de la Société d'Encouragement pour l'Industrie Nationale"* Paris 1820 (19th Year) p274

[235] http://*archives.marne.fr* Reims *Décès* 1822 2E 534/496 (Accessed April 2014)

[236] http://*archives.marne.fr* Châlons-en-Champagne *Décès* 1822 2E 119/388 (Accessed April 2014)

[237] http://*archives.marne.fr* Châlons-en-Champagne *Décès* 1835 2E 119/402 (Accessed April 2014)

[238] Chabal Family papers

[239] *"Un Bienfaiteur de l'Humanité"* by Katherine Golden Bitting 1924, USA, p15. Available online at http://babel.hathitrust.org/cgi/pt?id=wu. 89047913611;view =1up;seq=19 (Accessed April 2014)

[240] *"Annales Maritimes et Coloniales"* Paris 1822 *Tome II* p498 edited by M. Bajot

[241] *"Bulletin de la Société d'Encouragement pour l'Industrie Nationale"* Paris 1822 (21st Year) p230-233

[242] *"Les Artisans Illustres"* Édouard Foucaud, Paris 1841, p631

[243] "The Literary Gazette and Journal of the Belles Lettres, Arts, Sciences, Etc for the Year 1820" London 1820 p506 (No. 185, dated 5 August 1820)

[244] Ibid. p830 (No. 205, dated 23 December 1820)

[245] *"Le Livre de Tous Les Ménages ou L'Art de Conserver, pendant plusieurs années, toutes les substances animales et végétales"* by Nicolas Appert, Paris 1831 p187-189

[246] Ibid. Plate 2 Figure 3

[247] Ibid. p189

[248] Ibid. p190

[249] Ibid. p viij

[250] Ibid. p222

[251] Ibid. p222 – 224

[252] *"Description des machines et procédés spécifiés dans les brevets d'invention"* By M. Christian, *Tome XV*, Paris 1828 p305f

[253] *Archives Nationales* F12 2384 25 February 1822, cited in "Nicolas Appert" by Jean-Paul Barbier 1994 Royer p155 and note 14 p183

[254] *"Bulletin de la Société d'Encouragement pour l'Industrie Nationale"* Paris 1824 (23rd Year) p91 – 93

[255] *"Archives Des Découvertes et Des Inventions Nouvelles Pendant l'Année 1824"* Paris 1825 p470

[256] *"Bulletin de la Société d'Encouragement pour l'Industrie Nationale"* Paris 1824 (23rd Year) p303 – 305

[257] *"Revue Encyclopédique ou Analyse Raisonneé des Productions Les Plus Remarquables"Tome XXIV* Paris October 1824 p843f

[258] "The Literary Gazette and Journal of Belles Lettres, Arts, Sciences, Etc" London 1824 27 November 1824 p764

[259] *"Bulletin de la Société d'Encouragement pour l'Industrie Nationale"* Paris 1824 (23rd Year) p379

[260] "Nicolas Appert" by Jean-Paul Barbier 1994 Royer p155

[261] *Archives Nationales* F12 2432 16 February 1825, cited in "Nicolas Appert" by Jean-Paul Barbier 1994 Royer p155 – 156 and note 15 p183

[262] http://*archives.marne.fr* Châlons 1825 *Décès* 2E 119/391 (Accessed April 2014)

[263] *"La France Littéraire, ou Dictionnaire Bibliographique"* Paris 1830 by J-M Quérard, *Tome Quatrième* p450

[264] Entry on *Mme Lainé* in *"Rapport du Jury Central sur Les Produits de l'Industrie Française"*on the *Exposition* of 1827, Paris 1827, p416

[265] Ibid. p412

[266] *"Le Livre de Tous Les Ménages ou L'Art de Conserver, pendant plusieurs années, toutes les substances animales et végétales"* by Nicolas Appert, Paris 1831 p201

[267] Ibid. Plate 4

[268] Ibid. p200-209

[269] Ibid p215-219

[270] Photograph by Jean-Paul Barbier, downloaded from http://en.wikipedia.org/wiki/File:Malataverne_appert_jpb201005.JPG (Accessed April 2014) – free to use under Creative Commons

[271] *"Le Livre de Tous Les Ménages ou L'Art de Conserver, pendant plusieurs années, toutes les substances animales et végétales"* by Nicolas Appert, Paris 1831 p2-5

[272] Ibid. Plate 2

[273] Ibid. p29-30

[274] Ibid. p36-38

[275] "The Book of Illustrious Mechanics, of Europe and America" by Edward Foucaud, translated from the French, New York 1847 p342

[276] *"Le Livre de Tous Les Ménages ou L'Art de Conserver, pendant plusieurs années, toutes les substances animales et végétales"* by Nicolas Appert, Paris 1831 Plate 3

[277] Chambers's Edinburgh Journal Volume 18 No. 460, 23 October 1852 p259

[278] Chabal family papers

[279] *Archives de la Seine* Paris *Décès* 25 June 1828; Will at *Archives nationales* CX1/257. Also "Nicolas Appert" by Jean-Paul Barbier 1994 Royer p68 Note 9

[280] *"Bulletin de la Société d'Encouragement pour l'Industrie Nationale"* Paris 1830 (29th Year) p70

[281] Ibid. p175-176

[282] *"Le Livre de Tous Les Ménages ou L'Art de Conserver, pendant plusieurs années, toutes les substances animales et végétales"* by Nicolas Appert, Paris 1831 p i – iij

[283] Ibid. p x

[284] *"Bulletin de la Société d'Encouragement pour l'Industrie Nationale"* Paris 1831 (30th Year) p470f

[285] *Archives nationales* F12 2384, cited in "Nicolas Appert" by Jean-Paul Barbier 1994 Royer note 26 on p184

[286] "Nicolas Appert" by Jean-Paul Barbier 1994 Royer p172

[287] Ibid.

[288] *Archives nationales* F7 2485, cited in "Nicolas Appert" by Jean-Paul Barbier 1994 Royer p172 and note 27 on p184

[289] This date was given in the Appert dispay rooms in the Goethe/Schiller Museum in Châlons en Champagne. In Chabal family papers, the date is believed to be 4 July 1833.

[290] http://canadp-archivesenligne.paris.fr/archives_etat_civil *Etat civil reconstitué (XVIe siècle – 1859)*, Paris Marriages Appert 1833 (Accessed April 2014)

[291] archives.marne.fr *Décès* 1835 Châlons-sur-Marne 2E 119/402

[292] *Archives de la Seine* DQ 18-28, cited in "Nicolas Appert" by Jean-Paul Barbier 1994 Royer p174 and note 29 on p184

[293] "Nicolas Appert" by Jean-Paul Barbier 1994 Royer p176

[294] Ibid. and in notes 34 and 35 on p185

[295] Census details for Massy on archinoe.net 1836 6M 187

[296] *Journal de la Marne, juin* 1841. Quoted in "Nicolas Appert" by Jean-Paul Barbier 1994 Royer, p176 and note 36 on p185

[297] archinoe.net *Archives départementales de l'Essonne Naissances, mariages et décès* Massy 1840 – 1845 4E 1945

[298] "Nicolas Appert" by Jean-Paul Barbier 1994 Royer p178 and in note 39 on p185 quoting evidence from researches carried out in Massy in 1893

[299] Quoted in "Nicolas Appert" by Jean-Paul Barbier 1994 Royer p178

[300] Ibid.

[301] The work is out of copyright and the image occurs in many places online

[302] Saint-Julien-de-Civry *Publications de mariage* 1843 – 1852 5E 433/6

List of Illustrations

Index

Printed in Great Britain
by Amazon

23746260R00155